THE ROYAL TOUR: 1939

Arrival of Their Majesties, King George VI and Queen Elizabeth at the Parliament Buildings in Ottawa, May 19, 1939.

THE ROYAL TOUR of KING GEORGE VI and QUEEN ELIZABETH

in CANADA and the UNITED STATES of AMERICA

1939

by
Gustave Lanctot, K.C., D.Litt., LL.D.

E. P. TAYLOR FOUNDATION, Toronto

DEDICATED TO THE MEMORY OF

HIS LATE MAJESTY

KING GEORGE VI

PREFACE

FOR THE CANADA of today and tomorrow, the year 1939 will remain memorable for the visit of Their Majesties George VI and Elizabeth. For the first time in history, a British Sovereign was setting foot in America. Not less spectacular, the royal tour marked the first visit of a British King to the United States, when King George and Queen Elizabeth became the guests of President and Mrs. Roosevelt.

In accordance with the King's wish at the time, not to present a bare narrative of official functions, this account, while remaining documentary, aims at giving a living picture of the royal journey, visualizing both the personalities of the Sovereigns and the character of the welcome that greeted them everywhere from the day they landed until the day they sailed home.

The author was the official historian of the royal tour. Before his full account could be published, however, September 1939 intervened. It was not until 1963, when the E. P. Taylor Foundation learned of it, that the publication of the account was undertaken. Because of the lapse of time since the tour, it was decided that an abridged version would be more appropriate than the complete one. The condensation and editing have been done by Mrs. Barbara Urquhart. In order to retain as much as possible of the variety of incidents that marked the royal tour and to focus attention on the two central figures and the warmth of their welcome, details of some of the banquets and similar formal occasions were the first items to be omitted. Next were certain recurring events that can be summarized here: after leaving each city where they had stopped, the King had a message sent back to the mayor, expressing the warm appreciation of himself and the Queen for the hospitality extended by the city. The premier of each province received a similar telegram. The mayor of each city was also given a signed photograph of Their Majesties.

The fact that only the main stops are recounted in this edition must not be construed as any reflection on the welcome given by smaller towns and villages. All across the Dominion, wherever the royal train stopped even for five minutes—and at scores of places where it had to steam through without stopping—people came from miles around to express their affection and loyalty: feelings that were transmuted, by the very occasion of their expression, from an 'almost mystical reverence' (to use Lord Snell's words) for the Crown into a warmly personal attachment for their very human Majesties King George and Queen Elizabeth.

PROLOGUE

IT WAS APPARENTLY in early 1937 that a royal visit to Canada was first suggested. The idea probably grew out of the knowledge that at his coming Coronation George VI was to assume the additional title of King of Canada. Among others, the Canadian High Commissioner, Mr. Vincent Massey, did not fail to mention it at the proper opportunity. In May, when in London for the Coronation, the Prime Minister, Mr. Mackenzie King, took the opportunity to present to the King an official invitation to visit Canada.

The proposal greatly pleased His Majesty, but with troubles in Palestine and civil war in Spain, the time did not appear auspicious for his absence from London. Though the time was still far from reassuring in early 1938, with occupation of Austria by Germany, Canada's invitation was renewed through the Governor General, Lord Tweedsmuir, during a visit to England in June. As the international situation eased during the summer, the British Prime Minister, Mr. Neville Chamberlain, came to approve of a royal journey to Canada.

Already a favourable development had taken place. On August 8, 1938, President Roosevelt had come to Kingston to receive the honorary degree of LL.D. from Queen's University. While driving to Ivy Lea to open the new international bridge over the St. Lawrence, Mr. Mackenzie King informed the President of the King's projected coming to Canada. A week later, the President wrote in his own hand the yet unpublished letter to King George that follows:

August 25, 1938

My dear King George:
When I was in Canada a few days ago, Prime Minister Mackenzie King told me, in confidence, that there is a possibility that you and Her Majesty will visit the Dominion of Canada in the summer of 1939.

If this visit should become a reality, I hope very much that you will extend your visit to include the United States. I need not assure you that it would give my wife and me the greatest pleasure to see you, and, frankly, I think it would be an excellent thing for Anglo-American relations if you could visit the United States.

As you know, an International Exposition is to be held in New York City (and another one in San Francisco) in 1939. Doubtless you would not be able to visit both of them, but if you could come from Montreal or Ottawa to New York, it would be only an overnight journey.

If you should be here in June or July you might care to avoid the heat of Washington, and in such a case it would give us the greatest pleasure to have you and Her Majesty come to visit us at our country home at Hyde Park, which is on the Hudson River, about eighty miles north of New York, and, therefore, on the direct route between New York City and Canada. Also, it occurs to me that a Canadian trip would be crowded with formalities and that you both might like three or four days of very simple country life at Hyde Park—with no formal entertainments and an opportunity to get a bit of rest and relaxation.

In case you would like to come to Washington, however, and to see the Capitol, you would, of course, stay with us at the White House. This would of necessity be somewhat more formal, and, in the event that the Congress is still in session, there would probably be great pressure for you to be received by the Congress.

You and I are fully aware of the demands of the Protocol people, but, having had much experience with them, I am inclined to think that you and Her Majesty should do very much as you personally want to do—and I will see to it over here that your decision becomes the right decision.

I have had, as you know, the great privilege of knowing your splendid father, and I have also known two of your brothers. Therefore, I am greatly looking forward to the possibility of meeting you and the Queen.

There is, of course, no hurry about plans for next year, but I want you to know how sincerely welcome you would be if you could arrange to come to the United States.

I am asking Mr. Kennedy to give you this, but I think that we can keep any talk of your visit out of diplomatic channels for the time being. Your Ambassador, Ronald Lindsay, is a very old and close personal friend of mine, and he, I am sure, will understand.

I forgot to mention that if you bring either or both of the children with you, they will also be very welcome, and I shall try to have one or two Roosevelts of approximately the same age to play with them!

With my sincere regards,

Faithfully yours,

FRANKLIN D. ROOSEVELT

To this cordial letter, handed to him personally by the American Ambassador, Mr. Joseph Kennedy, King George answered by the following warm dispatch:

BALMORAL CASTLE

8th October, 1938

My dear President Roosevelt:

Your letter, which Mr. Kennedy handed to me last week, came as a pleasant relief at a time of great anxiety, and I thank you warmly for it.

The Queen and I appreciate most sincerely your kind invitation to visit Mrs. Roosevelt and you in the United States in the event of our going to Canada next summer. I can assure you that the pleasure, which it would in any case give to us personally, would be greatly enhanced by the thought that it was contributing in any way to the cordiality of the relations between our two countries.

I hope that it will not be inconvenient if I delay my answer until the plans for a visit to Canada are further advanced, and I am in a position to judge how long it may be possible for me to be absent from this country. I will then communicate with you again.

Although the suggestions which you make for a visit sound very attractive, I am afraid that we shall not be taking the children with us if we go to Canada, as they are much too young for such a strenuous tour.

Before I end this letter, I feel that I must say how greatly I welcomed your interventions in the recent crisis. I have little doubt that they contributed largely to the preservation of peace.

With all good wishes and many thanks for your kind invitation,

Believe me,

Yours very sincerely,

GEORGE, R.I.

It was under these circumstances that, on September 28, His Majesty informed Lord Tweedsmuir that he and the Queen proposed to visit Canada in the spring of 1939.

On February 16, a communication was issued from Buckingham Palace giving the names of the British official staff chosen to accompany Their Majesties to Canada:

Lady Nunburnholme and Lady Katharine Seymour, ladies-in-waiting; the Earl Eldon, lord-in-waiting to the King; the Earl of Airlie, Lord-Chamberlain to the Queen; Alan F. Lascelles, acting private secretary to the King; Surgeon Captain H. E. Y. White, R.N., medical officer; George F. Steward, chief press liaison officer; Captain Michael Adeane, assistant private secretary to the King; Lieutenant-Colonel the Honourable Piers Legh and Commander Abel Smith, R.N., equerries to the King.

Since it has been customary for the King to be accompanied by one of his constitutional advisers, as Minister in attendance, it appeared essential that the duty of serving as Minister in attendance upon His Majesty should be discharged by the Canadian Prime Minister. To assist him and the royal party, the following Canadian staff was appointed to be in attendance throughout the journey:

E. H. Coleman, K.C., LL.D., Under-Secretary of State and Chairman of the Interdepartmental Committee on the Royal Visit; Gustave Lanctot, K.C., D. Litt., LL.D., Dominion Archivist and Historian of the Royal Tour; Briga-dier S. T. Wood, Commissioner, Royal Canadian Mounted Police; Major-General H. H. Matthews, C.M.G., D.S.O., Adjutant General; A. D. P. Heeney, M.A., B.C.L., Principal Secretary to the Prime Minister; H. L. Keenleyside, M.A., Ph.D., Secretary of the Interdepartmental Committee on the Royal Visit; Brigadier-General Edouard deB. Panet, C.M.G., D.S.O., Member of the Secretariat; W. J. Turnbull, press liaison officer; Colonel C. H. King, Assistant Commissioner, Royal Canadian Mounted Police. Two members from the staff of Government House completed the group: A. S. Redfern, Secretary to the Governor General, and Lieutenant-Colonel E. D. Mackenzie, C.M.G., D.S.O., Comptroller of the Household.

To commemorate the royal visit, special stamps were issued, and a new silver dollar was struck by the Royal Canadian Mint.

On May 6, greeted on the way to Waterloo Station by thousands of spectators, Their Majesties boarded the train for Portsmouth. The old seaport crowds acclaimed the royal travellers with cheers. The King and Queen took leave of their children, the Queen saying to Princess Elizabeth: 'Be good and look after Margaret.' At three o'clock, the *Empress of Australia* moved out of the harbour on her way to Canada.

Several periods of fog delayed the progress of the ship, and it was only after ten days of sailing that the *Empress* reached Father Point on May 16. After picking up the river pilot, she proceeded on her course to Quebec, greeted on the way by bonfires on both banks of the St. Lawrence.

QUEBEC CITY

FOR CANADA the great festive day had arrived. On May 17, at Wolfe's Cove, the *Empress of Australia* berthed opposite the landing enclosure carpeted in red and green. Surrounded by a mass of spectators, the space was brightly coloured with draperies and banked with flowers and palms. Prime Minister Mackenzie King and the Minister of Justice, Honourable E. Lapointe, went on board the royal yacht and were conducted to the main lounge, where Their Majesties were waiting. The Prime Minister greeted the King and Queen and after a brief chat took leave of Their Majesties and returned to the quay.

At 10:34 a.m., just ahead of the Queen, George VI stepped off the gangway onto Canadian soil, the first British Sovereign to set foot in America. A royal salute of twenty-one guns began to boom from the Citadel, while His Majesty with the Prime Minister and Her Majesty with the Honourable Mr. Lapointe walked to the royal dais.

After the Prime Minister had presented to Their Majesties the various dignitaries who were assembled, the King inspected the guard of honour, formed by the Royal 22nd Regiment in scarlet coats and busbies, the only all-French regiment under the British King. Their Majesties then entered the royal automobile and proceeded towards the waiting city amidst waves of cheering spectators.

At 11:10, the royal car stopped in front of the Legislative Buildings, where the Sovereigns were greeted at the main entrance by the Lieutenant-Governor and Madame Patenaude, who presented to the Queen a bouquet of red roses. They walked to the Legislative Council's Red Chamber, hung with rich draperies and decorated with bowers of roses, where several hundred guests were already assembled.

When Their Majesties were seated on their thrones at the upper end of the Chamber, with the Prime Minister standing to the right of the King, Premier Duplessis, on behalf of the sole French Legislature of the British Empire, read

1

in French an address of welcome which expressed to the Sovereigns 'the sentiments of joy, respect, loyalty and affection of the entire Province of Quebec and, in particular, of Canadians of French descent'.

Upon receiving the Quebec address, His Majesty handed the Premier his reply, written in French. In it the King paid a special tribute to the well-established loyalty of the French-Canadian people.

Mayor Lucien Borne of Quebec also presented to His Majesty an address of welcome.

When the King and Queen walked out of the Chamber, the whole assembly broke spontaneously into warm applause. A short drive brought Their Majesties to the old Citadel, where Boy Scouts and Girl Guides formed a cheering cordon along the winding cobble-stone road of the fortress. From the flagstaff of the highest bastion, the Royal Standard shot its red and gold colours into the Laurentian sky: the King was in residence in Canada.

Being ahead of the programme schedule, Their Majesties enjoyed a rest, looking round their first Canadian home and admiring the wonderful panorama, which stretched across the sun-shot St. Lawrence, the green Island of Orleans, and the distant, bluish Laurentides.

At the Citadel, His Majesty performed his first official duty as King of Canada. The Prime Minister, as Secretary of State for External Affairs, laid before the King his recommendation for His Majesty's approval of the appointment of Daniel C. Roper as Envoy Extraordinary and Minister Plenipotentiary of the United States of America to Canada. The King signed the document, according to usage, in the top left-hand corner.

At one o'clock, Their Majesties left the Citadel and proceeded to the Château Frontenac for the luncheon given by the Dominion Government. In the banquet room, with its abundance of roses and delphinia, the three hundred distinguished guests were already in their places. They included not only the Cabinet Ministers, but also nearly all the members of the Privy Council for Canada and their wives, the Judges of the Supreme Court and their wives, and high officials of the Dominion.

At the conclusion of the lunch, the Prime Minister rose and delivered a speech welcoming Their Majesties to their Dominion of Canada:

> May it please Your Majesty:
>   On behalf of the Canadian people, I respectfully extend to Your Majesty and to Her Majesty the Queen a royal welcome to your Dominion of Canada.
>   We are deeply conscious of the signal honour of being the first of the overseas nations of the Commonwealth to be visited by the reigning

Sovereign, and of having the high privilege of welcoming, in person, our King and Queen. We are proud indeed to feel that, in the person of Your Majesty, we have among us, not the symbol, but the living presence of the Head of the whole Empire.

Three and a third centuries ago, unknown, unheralded and unwelcomed, a small craft crossed the then uncharted seas and sailed up the St. Lawrence to where this morning Your Majesty set foot on Canadian soil. Here, these early adventurers raised the fleur-de-lis of France and planted the Cross of Christianity. That day was the birthday of Canada. Since then, these heights have witnessed other scenes alike heroic and historic.

This afternoon Your Majesty will view the plains where one and three-quarter centuries ago the soil of Old France in the New World was won for the British Crown. The transition gave a firm foundation to the British dominions beyond the seas. Your Majesty will also see the memorial which, in a single epitaph, commemorates the virtues of the gallant leaders of the two great races then in conflict—a symbol of the highest chivalry, but, even more, of national unity.

Here, in 1864, after a preliminary conference at Charlottetown, the Fathers of Confederation drafted the resolutions which were the basis of the British North America Act. By this Act, the Provinces of Canada, Nova Scotia, and New Brunswick were federally united under the Crown into one Dominion. On July 1, 1867, with a constitution similar in principle to that of the United Kingdom, the British Colonies thus united became the Dominion of Canada.

To aid and advise in the government of the Dominion, the new constitution made provision for a Council to be styled the Queen's Privy Council for Canada.

Today, all the Privy Councillors of Canada have been invited to meet Your Majesty, including members of both present and past administrations. It is the first occasion since Confederation, apart from the meetings of the first Cabinet, on which all the members of the King's Privy Council for Canada have been brought together. It is the first time in the history of Canada that the Ministers of the Crown and, indeed, all members of Your Majesty's Privy Council, have been assembled in the presence of their King.

Today, as never before, the Throne has become the centre of our national life.

Under the shadow of the great rock of Quebec, there has passed, in the course of years, a continuous stream of men and women, seeking and finding new homes and new opportunities in this favoured land. We rejoice in the thought that, for a time, our King and Queen will follow the path of those adventurers and pioneers. Your Majesties will discover not only— as they did—forests, prairies, and mountains, but thriving villages, towns, and cities, all eager to extend their welcome. We hope there may be opportunity as well for Your Majesties to see and to enjoy something of the natural beauty of Canada's many rivers and lakes, its vast spaces, its clear skies and golden sunshine, its national parks, its quiet countryside and its peaceful homes.

We are not unmindful of the sacrifices involved in your long and arduous journeys over land and sea and in parting for the time being with your children—those cherished children of the Empire, the Princesses Elizabeth and Margaret Rose. May the sincerity and warmth of our welcome be some compensation to you during this temporary separation. Your Majesties will find other children in this land longing to press around you, children who in turn will hand on to a future generation the memory of a great moment in their lives. Here, too, you will be in the heart of a family which is your own: a family of men and women of varied stock and race and thought, who, in free association with other members of the Commonwealth, but equally in their own way, are working out their national destiny.

We would have Your Majesties feel that, in coming from the Old Land to the New, you have but left one home to come to another: that we are all of one household. Free institutions and democratic ideals are as dear to the heart of your people in Canada as to the peoples in any other part of the Empire. We regard their preservation and perpetuation as the common concern of all.

May I, in conclusion, be permitted to say that the warmth of the welcome Your Majesties will everywhere receive is bound up in a very special way with the admiration that all Canadians feel for the qualities of heart and character which you possess, for what you are in yourselves. In your daily lives we see exemplified the things we value most: faith in God, concern for human well-being, consecration to the public service, delight in the simple joys of home and family life. Greater than our sense of the splendour of your state is our affection for two young people who bear, in so high a spirit, a responsibility unparalleled in the world.

Senator Dandurand, Government Leader in the Senate, made a short speech in French:

Qu'il plaise à Votre Majesté:

Pour vous souhaiter la bienvenue dans la capitale de la Nouvelle-France, fondée en 1608 par Champlain et ses héroïques compagnons dont vous suivrez les traces jusqu'aux contreforts des Montagnes-Rocheuses, la voix de leurs descendants s'impose, comme aussi pour solliciter la faveur de déposer aux pieds de votre charmante compagne le respectueux hommage de toute notre population. La race des découvreurs et des pionniers du Canada vous est d'autant moins inconnue que vous vous réclamez, Sire, et non sans fierté, d'une commune, bien que lointaine, parenté.

En effet, ils sont directement issus de ce grand Duché de Normandie qui donna à son chef, Guillaume, cinquante mille hommes pour vaincre à Hastings et y établir sa domination sur l'Angleterre. C'est la progéniture de ces Anglo-normands qui est venue rejoindre ici même, en 1760, ses cousins franco-normands.

Ils ne parlaient plus tout a fait la même langue, car dans votre île, la langue avait sensiblement évolué au cours des siècles. Aussi éprouvèrent-ils, dès l'abord, quelque difficulté à se comprendre, bien que des milliers de vocables français eussent conservé leur forme. En particulier, deux mots avaient gardé leur aspect original et leur plein sens, deux mots qui restaient profondement gravés dans leur âme normande et qu'ils ne devaient jamais oublier, deux mots qu'ils retrouvèrent dans votre écusson royal: 'Dieu et mon Droit'.

C'est la fidélité indéfectible à ces deux principes essentiels de vie— 'Dieu et mon Droit'—qui a assuré leur survivance.

Sous l'égide de cette devise, ils ont pu clamer, en changeant d'allégeance, à l'instar des chevaliers du moyen âge: 'Le Roi est mort; vive le Roi!'

Aussi aujourd'hui répètent-ils à l'adresse de Votre Majesté, sans aucune réticence et de plein coeur: 'Vive le Roi!'

Then the King arose and, speaking feelingly, delivered an excellent address:

I am deeply moved by your words of welcome to the Queen and myself on behalf of the Canadian people.

I recognize that this moment is historic. It is the first time that a British king has crossed the Atlantic. I stand today on the soil of North America.

Here, in the past two centuries, through loss and through gain, the British Commonwealth of Nations has been largely moulded into its present form.

This is also the first visit of the Sovereign to one of his overseas dominions. It is fitting that it should be the senior dominion of the Crown. I am particularly pleased that, on the day of my arrival in Canada, I should have the pleasure of meeting, not only my Ministers, but all the leaders of my Privy Council in Canada.

You in Canada have already fulfilled part of the Biblical promise and obtained dominion from sea to sea. You are engaged in fulfilling the latter part of that promise in consolidating government from the river to the ends of the earth, from the St. Lawrence to the Arctic snows.

The Queen and I are looking forward, with anticipation too great for expression, to seeing all we possibly can of this vast country. Particularly do we welcome the opportunity of greeting the men and women who are its strength and stay, and of seeing something of the younger generation so soon to become the guardians of its future.

Je veux, Monsieur le sénateur Dandurand, saluer l'ancienne province de Québec et cette belle et ancienne cité, dans la langue des pionniers qui apportèrent la civilisation sur les rives du fleuve Saint-Laurent. C'est ici que s'ouvrit pour la première fois la porte du Canada, et que naquit la nation canadienne.

C'est ici que de grands exploits furent accomplis, laissant des témoign-
ages qui resteront à jamais glôrieux pour la France et la Grande-Bretagne.
C'est ici aujourd'hui que deux grandes races vivent ensemble et heureuses.
L'esprit de Québec est un heureux mélange d'esprit vigoureux et fièrement
maintenu.

C'est ici de cette vieille partie du Canada que partirent de nombreux
pionniers pour l'Ouest et le Nord-Ouest, où ils se joignirent aux fils des Iles
britanniques et des nations de l'Europe continentale pour faire du Canada
un pays d'hommes libres.

C'est l'union de l'ancien et du nouveau qui fait une cité ou une nation
puissante.

L'accord et l'union harmonieux des éléments variés qui forment le
Canada furent le rêve idéal des Pères de la Confédération. Je ne puis
souhaiter pour vous qui m'entendez un destin plus fortuné que la réalisa-
tion fructueuse et heureuse de ce noble rêve.

With the last words of the speech hardly spoken, the company burst out
in acclaim lasting several minutes. The Queen, joining in the applause, turned
to the King with a smile and was overheard to murmur: 'It was very good,
dear.'

Soon after the luncheon was over, Their Majesties entered their limousine
for a drive through the city. The moment the royal car came in sight of the
densely packed crowds, who had listened to the King's speech transmitted by
loudspeakers, cheers went up intermingled with the cries: 'Vive le Roi! Vive
la Reine!' The welcome was taken up and maintained along the nine-mile
route.

The triumphant parade came to a climax at the Battlefields Park. On the
vast stretch of the Plains of Abraham were congregated twenty-five thousand
school children, each holding a small flag, while thousands of spectators had
gathered in the background. When the royal car came to a stop, cheers rose
while a sea of flags fluttered madly in the air. Then twenty-five thousand
voices sang 'God Save the King' and then 'O Canada', both in French.

After three little girls, one French, one English, and one Irish, had presented to the Queen a bouquet of roses, a few leaders in education were
introduced to Their Majesties by Premier Duplessis. Their Majesties re-entered
their car, and a five-minute drive brought them to the Lieutenant-Governor's
residence, 'Spencerwood'. The King and Queen were met at the entrance by
the Lieutenant-Governor and Madame Patenaude and escorted to the reception rooms. Tea was served in the state dining-rooms. Before leaving, Their
Majesties presented Lieutenant-Governor and Madame Patenaude with their
autographed photographs.

From their Canadian residence, Their Majesties caused a thoughtful message to be sent out in appreciation of the numerous greetings received since their arrival in Canada. It read as follows:

> The King and Queen are deeply touched by the many messages of welcome and goodwill which have reached them on their arrival in Canada from all parts of the Dominion and from the United States. The volume of these messages is so great that it will not be possible for Their Majesties to answer them individually. They wish, however, to express to the senders their most sincere thanks for their good wishes.

At eight o'clock, the Sovereigns left the Citadel to attend the official dinner given by the Quebec Government at the Château Frontenac. Their Majesties were received at the main entrance by Prime Minister King and Premier Duplessis. With no formal address, the provincial dinner resolved itself into a brilliant social function chiefly centred on Her Majesty, radiant and regal. On the conclusion of the dinner, the toasts to the King and then to the Queen were proposed by Lieutenant-Governor Patenaude. The King and Queen arose, bowing and smiling, and the toast was duly honoured.

A few minutes later the royal party walked to the foyer, where a few distinguished guests were presented to them; they chatted with this group for about ten minutes, after which they were escorted to their car by Prime Minister Mackenzie King and Premier Duplessis. Outside, in spite of a drizzle, the crowd was jamming the whole square, occasionally calling: 'Le Roi! La Reine!' As Their Majesties drove off to their Canadian home at the Citadel, the people cheered.

At the same time, visible from the royal windows, a fireworks display across the river at Lévis lit up the sky with shooting rockets and sparkling flares. So ended the Sovereigns' first day in Canada.

QUEBEC CITY–TROIS RIVIÈRES

NEXT MORNING, May 18, the Sovereigns arose early, and at nine o'clock they left the Citadel for the railway station. At the station they were met by Lieutenant-Governor Patenaude, Premier Duplessis, and Mayor Borne. A royal salute was fired by the 94th Artillery Brigade from the St. Charles River. As the train pulled out, with the royal couple standing on the observation platform, the large crowd swept round the station to the tracks shouting, 'Vive le Roi! Vive la Reine!'

Now on board the train, a British King and his Queen, for the first time in history, were going to live for weeks in railway cars; a Canadian train thus became a 'Buckingham Palace on wheels'. On board also were ten British members of the royal staff and a retinue of twenty personal attendants. During the whole tour, the Sovereigns were accompanied by Prime Minister Mackenzie King, as His Majesty's constitutional adviser, and ten Canadian members of the royal party. To the train were attached thirty secretarial attendants, and railway officials and employees, as well as maids and valets.

The train consisted of twelve cars provided equally by the Canadian National Railways and the Canadian Pacific Railway; these coaches were painted royal blue, with silver panels between the windows and a horizontal gold stripe above and below the windows. The last two cars were occupied by the Sovereigns, and bore a royal coat of arms in gold in the centre, while the others had the royal cipher and crown. The last car contained a sitting-room for the Sovereigns and two bedrooms with dressing-rooms and private baths attached, as well as two bedrooms for members of the staff. The Queen's suite was painted blue-grey, with damask coverings and curtains of dusty pink. The King's rooms displayed blue and white chintz. The sitting-room contained a radio and a small library. There, also, a set of specially designed maps had been installed (rolling up and down like blinds) so that any place in Canada could be instantly located. A special milometer was also installed to indicate the distance travelled by the train.

The second-last car consisted of a large lounge and a dining-room seating twelve persons, with a kitchen attached; as well as a bedroom and an office for the King's private secretary.

At the personal command of the King, a buzzer system had been installed between the engine and the royal suite with instructions that whenever the engineer sighted a crowd of people at a station not marked for a stop, he was to press the buzzer and slow down, so that Their Majesties could appear on the observation platform.

The royal train was also provided with a post-office, using its own post-marks. All letters reaching or leaving the train passed through this office. All over America, there was such a tremendous rush to secure royal stamps bearing the cancellation mark of the royal train that one day 250,000 letters were mailed from the train, to which they had been sent for that purpose alone.

The royal train was preceded throughout the tour by another train known as the pilot train, travelling half an hour ahead of it, and carrying journalists, photographers, and radiomen, relief Mounted Policemen, and postal, telegraph, and telephone officials.

Life on board the royal train ran smoothly, with a minimum of regulation. The King and Queen spent most of their time in their drawing-room conversing or reading, listening to the radio, or occasionally playing a game of patience.

Leaving Quebec City, the royal train sped away through the countryside. All along the route, sturdy farmers and their wives had gathered at cross-roads or at stations. They had come on foot, in buggies, in farm wagons, in cars, or in trucks. Each little station had its decorations. These people had come to catch a view of the royal train with practically no hope of seeing the King and Queen themselves. They cheered even when the blue train steamed past without a glimpse of the Sovereigns through the windows. But the cheers rose louder and longer when the train slowed down and the King and Queen appeared on the observation platform. At most stations a special place was reserved for school children.

Before the train reached Trois-Rivières, Premier Duplessis, who was travelling in the Prime Minister's car, was invited to the royal car, and the King presented to him signed photographs of Their Majesties.

The moment the train came to a halt at Trois-Rivières, the Sovereigns alighted from their car and the Prime Minister presented to the King and Queen Mayor and Madame Pitt. Then the party walked to a dais, beside which the Trois-Rivières Tank Regiment was drawn up as a guard of honour. In the open space on each side a crowd of over fifty thousand people, as closely

jammed as could be, had filled every inch of room. At Their Majesties' appearance, roaring cheers rose from the multitude. The Queen smiled and waved
her hand while the King saluted. Mayor Pitt handed to the King the city's
address of welcome. Premier Duplessis and Mayor Pitt having taken their
leave, Their Majesties returned to the royal train and stood on the observation
platform, waving to the cheering crowd while the train pulled out of Trois-
Rivières.

MONTREAL

AT QUARTER PAST TWO the royal train pulled into Jean Talon Station in
Montreal. Never before had such multitudes gathered in a Canadian city.
Even before daybreak, people had begun to pour into the city from all over
the surrounding region, while thousands—including a large contingent from
the United States—had come a day or two ahead. From early morning, small
groups, often with folding stools, steamer rugs, or lunch baskets, had streamed
along the streets, while thousands of school children marched to their
appointed stations. Open spaces along the streets were occupied by grandstands.

At the station, gay with streamers, the Sovereigns alighted and walked to
the dais while a royal salute was fired by the 2nd Montreal Regiment. The
Prime Minister presented the Mayor of Montreal. His Majesty inspected the
guard of honour, comprised of soldiers of the Fusiliers Mont-Royal and the
Black Watch of Canada. The inspection over, Their Majesties entered the
royal motor-car and the whole procession moved off, a detachment of the
Duke of York's Royal Canadian Hussars escorting the royal automobile.

The twenty-three-mile drive through the city was a triumphant progress
between walls of cheering humanity waving and shouting. Over one million
people were packed along the curbs and in public squares, or crowded on
stands and in vacant lots. The route was resplendent and colourful with
innumerable decorations. Escorted by the hussars and warmly applauded by
swarming spectators, the royal visitors traversed Outremont and the city's

East End. There the royal automobile drove into the Montreal Stadium, where 40,000 French-Canadian boys and girls were seated, one thousand of them dressed in red, white, and blue capes to form a huge Union Jack. When the big maroon car flying the Royal Standard slowly rolled in, a stupendous cheer burst forth. Then rose the French words of the National Anthem in youthful, stirring tones.

Later on, the royal cortège passed a stand packed with girls and boys all dressed in black. They eagerly waved their flags, but did not cheer. They were deaf and dumb pupils of a neighbouring school.

Next, the procession headed for the Jacques Cartier Bridge spanning the river, from which the Sovereigns were afforded a splendid view of Montreal harbour. Reversing its route, the royal car came to a halt at the City Hall, which was gorgeously draped in red, gold, and blue.

With trumpets blaring outside, Their Majesties entered, escorted by Mayor and Madame Houde, and the Prime Minister. His Majesty was presented with an address of welcome by the Mayor. After the King and Queen had signed the city's 'Livre d'or', the aldermen and a few prominent citizens and their wives were presented to Their Majesties by the Mayor. The following five holders of the Victoria Cross, resident in Montreal, were also presented: Air Marshal W. A. Bishop, Lieutenant-Colonel W. H. Clark-Kennedy, Lieutenant-Colonel W. T. Macdowell, Captain C. N. Mitchell, and Corporal Tombs.

At the close of the reception, the Sovereigns resumed their drive, through crowded streets and McGill University campus, to Molson Stadium, where, to the delighted cheers of 14,000 children of the Montreal English schools, the car proceeded slowly around the track. Then, passing through the western section of the city, the procession went up the wooded Shakespeare Road, closely lined with cheering Boy Scouts and Girl Guides. Farther up, Remembrance Road—in honour of Canada's Great War dead—was officially opened by Their Majesties as their car, the first to traverse it, snapped a ribbon stretched across the street. The drive brought the royal party to the Chalet on the top of Mount Royal. Their Majesties strolled onto the balcony with Mayor Houde and the Prime Minister; and, standing on almost the same spot as Jacques Cartier four centuries ago, they admired the immense panorama of Montreal with its lofty church spires and tall buildings, stretching along the broad St. Lawrence, with three isolated mountains in the background. The King unveiled a simple granite block, erected to commemorate the royal visit.

Presently the Sovereigns re-entered their car to drive through residential

Westmount, ablaze with flags and streamers, the crowds acclaiming Their Majesties. On Sherbrooke Street the procession passed a large group of Caughnawaga Indians drawn up round a totem pole with two banners bearing the inscription: 'Welcome to the Great White Father and Mother'. Next the royal car brought Their Majesties to Windsor Station and the royal train. On reaching the station, the King gave instructions to send to Mayor Houde autographed portraits of Their Majesties.

At eight o'clock in the evening, Their Majesties drove to the Hotel Windsor to attend the dinner given in their honour by the City of Montreal. Received by Mayor and Madame Houde, the Sovereigns agreed to appear on the balcony overlooking Dominion Square, where an immense multitude of spectators had gathered. As the King and Queen came into full view, a thunderous roar of applause surged up.

Presently Their Majesties entered the flower-decked and brilliantly decorated banquet hall, where half of the one thousand guests were waiting; the other half of the company had to be accommodated in the adjoining Rose Room.

At a moment during the banquet when conversation had flagged somewhat, the King, noticing that Mayor Houde was fidgeting with a piece of paper in his hand, asked, 'What's that you have there, Mr. Mayor?'—'Sir, it is a list of what I must do and not do this evening.'—'May I see it?'—'Yes, Sir, but it will make me blush.'

Mayor Houde then handed over the notes, which were in French; and, with the Queen listening, the King read them out, item by item, with great amusement. 'Did you do this?' the King asked.—'Yes, Your Majesty, I did.' —'But you certainly did not do this,' said the King, enjoying himself completely.—'I am afraid you have got me there, Sir,' admitted Mayor Houde, 'but if you wish, I shall start it all over again.' And Their Majesties broke into hearty laughter, as did also the Mayor, who added, 'I wish I could talk, but I am supposed to wait until I am spoken to.'—'Mr. Mayor, I am your King, and I order you tell me what you like.' And so, leaving formality aside, Mr. Houde kept the royal guests in continuous merriment with his witty sallies and droll stories, some in French and some in English.

Before the dessert, the Mayor proposed the King's and the Queen's health in the two languages.

Outside, in Dominion Square, the immense crowd which had been waiting for over an hour and a half started to chant out, 'We want the King! We want the Queen!' Soon the chant grew into a roar so persistent that word of the popular wish was brought to Mayor Houde. He mentioned it to the King, and most graciously Their Majesties agreed at once to make an appearance in public. Accompanied by Mayor Houde and the Prime Minister, they made their way to the balcony overlooking the square. In this vast place was a solid mass of humanity—perhaps a hundred thousand spectators. The instant they appeared on the light-flooded balcony, the King and Queen were greeted with wave after wave of cheers from that waiting sea of humanity.

On leaving the balcony, the royal party returned to the banquet hall for dessert and coffee, but this time took their seats in the Rose Room in order to give the overflow guests the benefit of their presence. During the dinner, between selections by a string orchestra, English and French folk-songs were sung by a French-Canadian quartet. After a last song in the Rose Room, Mayor Houde rose and said, 'Her Majesty has told me that she is teaching Princesses Elizabeth and Margaret Rose our song: "Alouette". I shall ask the quartet to sing it for the Queen.' They did, with great success. The King beat time to the tune, the Queen hummed it with the necessary gestures to nose, head, and arms, and soon the whole company was singing it. The Queen then asked Mayor Houde what was the standing of 'Alouette' in Quebec. 'If Your Majesty allows me to be frank,' replied the Mayor, 'I'll say it is our national anthem after midnight.'

At 10:15 p.m. Their Majesties left the banquet. Stepping into their car amid cheers from the crowd in Dominion Square, they drove to Windsor Station. There the Sovereigns were greeted by Sir Edward Beatty and other directors of the Canadian Pacific Railway. As the train started to move, Their Majesties came to the observation platform smiling and waving their farewells to the cheering spectators filling the station. At the same time, a twenty-one-gun salute was fired from the Dorchester Street Bridge by the 2nd Montreal Regiment, R.C.A., while on the slopes of Mount Royal a display of fireworks was shooting into the sky Montreal's last salute to the royal visitors on their way to Ottawa. At Westmount Station, so great was the crowd that the Queen appeared in answer to the ovation; and still farther on, at Montreal West, the Sovereigns came out to acknowledge the cheers of five thousand persons, though it was by then close to midnight.

OTTAWA

FIRST DAY

FROM THE EARLY HOURS of the morning, thousands upon thousands had been pouring into Ottawa. At eleven o'clock, the engine drew to a halt at Island Park Station. When the King and Queen stepped down to the red-carpeted platform with its canopy draped in bunting, the crowd broke into great cheers, a royal salute of twenty-one guns was fired by the 1st Field Battery, R.C.A., and the band of the Cameron Highlanders played the National Anthem.

The Sovereigns were greeted by the Governor General and the Lady Tweedsmuir, who were accompanied by Cabinet Ministers, the Speakers of the Senate and of the House of Commons, and other prominent officials. The presentation over, the King went out to inspect the guard of honour formed by the Cameron Highlanders of Canada.

Their Majesties now entered the state landau. Accompanied by a mounted escort of the 4th Princess Louise Dragoon Guards, the royal coach moved ahead amid continuous applause. Island Park Drive was lined with soldiers, cadets, Boy Scouts (including a group of three hundred from northern New York State), and war veterans in berets. At Lansdowne Park ten thousand school children were assembled, as well as six hundred inmates of various hospitals and institutions, including many aged and crippled persons.

Attended now by a new escort formed by the Royal Canadian Dragoons, the state landau proceeded along the Driveway between solid lines of cheering spectators to Confederation Square, while from the Peace Tower on Parliament Hill the carillon pealed forth the nation's welcome. Round the War Memorial and along the converging streets, tall poles displayed heraldic banners, and flags and bunting decorated every building in sight. In that colourful setting were massed dense crowds of spectators roaring their homage and joy.

The last stage of the procession took Their Majesties to Government House, whose driveway was lined with cheering Boy Scouts and Girl Guides.

14

The royal landau came to a stop before Government House, over which had just been hoisted the Royal Standard, and in front of which sentries of the Royal Canadian Air Force stood guard. When Their Majesties walked into their Canadian residence, the Statute of Westminster had assumed full reality: the King of Canada had come home.

In the study an unprecedented ceremony took place, as a representative of a foreign government in Canada presented to the King himself the credentials usually delivered to the Governor General. His Majesty accepted the credentials of the new United States Minister to Canada, Daniel C. Roper, former Secretary for Commerce in the Roosevelt administration. After the ceremony, which was notable for the expressions of goodwill that were exchanged, the heads of the diplomatic missions were presented to the King.

Early in the afternoon the Sovereigns lunched privately at Government House with the Governor General and the Lady Tweedsmuir.

At half past two, Their Majesties left Government House in their covered car, escorted by a mounted detachment of the Princess Louise Dragoons, and drove to Parliament Hill. At the main entrance at the foot of the Peace Tower Their Majesties alighted and were greeted by the Prime Minister, who escorted the Queen into the building.

In the meantime, the stage had been set in the Senate Chamber for the greatest royal function of all. At two o'clock, the Speaker's procession entered the room, the Gentleman Usher of the Black Rod (Major A. R. Thompson) preceding Speaker Walter E. Foster, who was followed by the Clerk and the Assistant Clerk. The Speaker read the prayer. The Government Leader, Senator Dandurand, gave notice of a Bill which was given its three readings and passed; and then the Senate adjourned during pleasure. After an interval, during which the Lady Tweedsmuir entered and took her seat with a large party in the viceregal box (the Governor General was not present), the voice of an assistant announced: 'Order!', all present stood, and a hush fell upon the Red Chamber. Up the aisle went the procession, in the following order:

Honorary Aides-de-Camp to the Governor General
Field-Officer-in-Waiting

Commander E. M. C. Abel Smith,   Lieutenant-Colonel the Hon.
R.N., Equerry   P. W. Legh, Equerry

Captain M. Adeane, Assistant Secretary to the King

Major Andrew R. Thompson, The Gentleman Usher of the Black Rod

Mr. A. F. Lascelles, Acting Private Secretary to the King

The Earl of Airlie, Lord	The Earl of Eldon, Lord-
Chamberlain to the Queen	in-Waiting to the King

THE QUEEN   THE KING

Guy Coté,   Kenneth Greene,
Page   Page

Lady Nunburnholme, Lady-in-Waiting   The Prime Minister
Lady Katharine Seymour, Lady-in-Waiting   The Leader of the Senate

Members of the Defence Council
Associate Members of the Defence Council

Ending the procession, there followed in dress uniform twenty senior officers and officers commanding local military units.

With the King lightly holding the Queen's upraised hand, Their Majesties walked together, the King looking rather serious, and the Queen smiling to the company, who bowed as the Sovereigns passed in front of them. It was an impressive moment. Slowly, with a solemnity born of the dignity of centuries-old pageantry, mingling historic and present significance, the procession came to the foot of the throne, its members separating to right and left and grouping themselves on either side of the dais. His Majesty ascended the steps of the dais and stood before his chair on the left. The Queen then moved forward, taking her position before her chair on His Majesty's left. When the rest of the procession had taken their appointed places, the Gentleman Usher of the Black Rod said: 'Pray be seated', and all present sat down, save the members of the royal procession, who remained standing on either side of the dais.

The Speaker of the Senate arose from his seat facing the throne, and, raising his three-cornered hat, bowed to Their Majesties and said: 'Gentleman Usher of the Black Rod, you will proceed to the House of Commons and acquaint that House that it is His Majesty's pleasure that they attend him immediately in the Senate.'

After repeating this command in French, the Speaker bowed to His Majesty and resumed his seat.

The Gentleman Usher of the Black Rod, in accordance with tradition, walked down to the House of Commons and presently returned, followed by the Speaker and Members of the House of Commons, who took their places at the Bar of the Senate. The Gentleman Usher of the Black Rod called 'Order!', whereupon Speaker Casgrain raised his hat to His Majesty, who bowed in return.

Now the Assistant Clerk of the Senate, Dr. L. P. Gauthier, rose from beside the Speaker, bowed to His Majesty, and said: 'May it please Your Majesty, the Senate and House of Commons have passed the following Bills to which they humbly request Your Majesty's assent.' And he read the titles of eight Acts.

The Assistant Clerk then bowed to His Majesty and repeated the same words in French. Thereupon the Clerk of the Senate, Major L. C. Moyer, bowed to the King, and holding the Bills aloft in sight of the King, said in both English and French: 'His Majesty doth assent to these Bills', and His Majesty made an inclination of the head indicating assent.

With similar ceremony the King assented to the Supply Bill.

His Majesty then read his short speech:

Honourable Members of the Senate, Members of the House of Commons:

I thank you sincerely for your addresses received on my arrival at Quebec. The Queen and I deeply appreciate your loyal and affectionate messages.

I am very happy that my visit to Canada affords me the opportunity of meeting, in Parliament assembled, the members of both Houses. No ceremony could more completely symbolize the free and equal association of the nations of our Commonwealth. As my father said, on the occasion of his Silver Jubilee, the unity of the British Empire is no longer expressed by the supremacy of the time-honoured Parliament that sits at Westminster. It finds expression today in the free association of nations enjoying common principles of government, a common attachment to ideals of peace and freedom, and bound together by a common allegiance to the Crown.

The Queen and I have been deeply touched by the warmth of the welcome accorded us since our arrival in Canada. We are greatly looking forward to visiting each of the provinces and, before our return, to paying a brief visit to the United States.

It is my earnest hope that my present visit may give my Canadian people a deeper conception of their unity as a nation. I hope also that my visit to the United States will help to maintain the very friendly relations existing between that great country and the nations of the Commonwealth.

These visits, like the one recently made by the Queen and myself to the continent of Europe, will, we trust, be viewed as an expression of the spirit of our peoples, which seek ardently for closer friendship and better relations not only with our kith and kin but with the peoples of all nations and races.

Honourable Members of the Senate, Members of the House of Commons:

May the blessing of Divine Providence rest upon your labours and upon my realm of Canada.

His Majesty then read the speech in French. Thus came to an end the most spectacular ceremony in the whole of Canadian history.

On the conclusion of the royal speech, the Speaker, preceded by the Sergeant-at-arms carrying the mace, and the members of the House of Commons, withdrew and returned to the Green Chamber. Now His Majesty being pleased to retire, the Gentleman Usher of the Black Rod stepped forward and bowed to the Sovereigns. All present stood, and the royal procession, re-forming itself, walked down the aisle in the same order as it had come in, the King and Queen again gracefully holding their upraised hands, while the audience bowed as they passed, which the Queen gracefully acknowledged with smiles to the right and left.

As Their Majesties appeared on the steps of the Peace Tower, the thousands assembled in front of the Parliament Buildings burst into prolonged cheering. The band struck up the National Anthem, and the King and Queen, in their regal attire, stood together, framed in the Gothic arch of the Tower under the soft blue of a Canadian sky.

On the conclusion of the Anthem, the Queen turned and shook hands with the Prime Minister and Senator Dandurand. The Sovereigns then entered the royal car and departed for Government House amidst renewed cheers, while the strains of 'God Save the King' pealed out from the carillon of the lofty Peace Tower.

After a quiet tea at Government House came a reception exclusively for newspapermen and women. On 'Their Majesties' commands', the Governor General had invited to a reception at Rideau Hall the newspaper correspondents on the royal pilot train, British, Canadian, and American, together with the members of the Parliamentary Press Gallery and the local newspapers. The reception proved informal and delightful. The one hundred and forty men and women present were drawn up in a circle when Their Majesties came in unannounced. The Chairman of the Publicity Committee of the royal tour, Walter S. Thompson, presented each guest in turn. First the Queen, and then the King, shook hands with everybody. Now and then they asked questions or stopped for a brief talk. All was done in a spirit of friendliness and a charm of manner that conquered everyone. The introductions over, Their Majesties, who seemed to enjoy this interviewing of interviewers, left the room with a smile to the company, who broke into spontaneous applause.

After the reception, the King and Lord Tweedsmuir enjoyed a brisk walk round the spacious grounds of Rideau Hall. But the respite was not long. Presently His Majesty received Prime Minister King, who in his capacity as Secretary of State for External Affairs laid before him the Trade Agreement between Canada and the United States, signed at Washington on November 17, 1938, and the Convention regarding the boundary waters of the Rainy Lake district between the two countries, signed at Ottawa on September 15, 1938. The King's ratification of these two agreements marked the first time that such ratification had been done under the Great Seal of Canada. (Previously it had been done under the Great Seal of Great Britain.) Thus a new official procedure was established, which asserted and recognized Canada's equality of political status within the British Empire. Then the King signed also the Bills to which he had signified approval in the Senate earlier in the afternoon.

A brilliant state banquet, given by the Governor General and the Lady Tweedsmuir in the ball-room at Government House, closed the most eventful day in the capital's history. The guests assembled in the Chinese Room. At 8:15 p.m. the Governor General and the Lady Tweedsmuir, attended by Lieutenant-Colonel E. D. Mackenzie, proceeded to Their Majesties' rooms and escorted them to the Chinese Room. The guests were then presented to Their Majesties, each guest after presentation moving to his place in the dining-room.

Lord Tweedsmuir occupied the centre seat at the top section of the horseshoe-shaped table, with the King to the right and the Queen to the left. On the King's right was seated the Lady Tweedsmuir, and on the Queen's left, Prime Minister King. After the dessert was served, pipers of the Cameron Highlanders of Ottawa piped round the dining-room; then Their Majesties left the room, followed by the guests.

OTTAWA

SECOND DAY

SATURDAY, MAY 20, had been appointed by proclamation as the day for honouring the King's birthday in Canada. It had been arranged to celebrate the occasion with the historic ceremony of the Trooping of the King's Colour, with His Majesty taking the salute.

Thousands of spectators crowded the streets and the spacious green lawns that face the Houses of Parliament. There already stood in full-dress uniform the two regiments of Canadian Guards selected to perform the ceremony.

At 10:15 His Majesty, attended by Major-General T. V. Anderson, Chief of the General Staff, entered an open car at Government House and, accompanied by a mounted escort of the Royal Canadian Dragoons, drove to Parliament Hill. He proceeded to the royal box on the edge of the central walk, his arrival being greeted with enthusiastic applause. Passing through the royal box, His Majesty moved forward a few yards and took his position at the saluting base. Composed of two regiments—the Governor General's Foot Guards and the Canadian Grenadier Guards—the brigade of Guards formed a hollow square, two ranks deep, of red and blue uniforms. The King stepped out, accompanied by Major-General Anderson, and, walking along the line, inspected the regiments, while the bands of the two regiments played 'Land of Hope and Glory'.

After taking the salute and inspecting the regiments, the King returned to the royal box, and took his place on the reviewing stand. Then began the imposing ceremony of the Trooping of the Colour. With the brigade 'at the present' and the band playing solemn music, the escort of the Colour moved out and came to a halt opposite the sentry-guarded stand on the lower end of the east lawn, where hanging on its staff was the King's Colour of the brigade of Guards, a flag of maroon and gold about five feet square. With an ensign holding it taut and high, the Colour was trooped down the line in slow time, and then in quick time.

When this first part of the ceremony was over, His Majesty moved from the royal box to the saluting base, and the brigade marched past the King in slow time, and then again in quick time. Each time, on coming to the base where His Majesty stood at the salute, the ensign carrying the Colour lowered it to the horizontal, the highest honour that can be rendered. After the march-past, the brigade presented arms to the King, while the Colour was lowered and the band played the National Anthem. Thus ended the brilliant pageant.

When the King returned to the royal box, the following Ottawa residents, holders of the Victoria Cross, were presented: Lieutenant-General Sir Richard E. W. Turner, Major Milton F. Gregg, Private P. Konowal, and Albert Hill, now of California.

After these presentations, the King, accompanied by the Prime Minister, walked from the royal box to his waiting car. At the private entrance of the Speaker of the Senate he was joined by the Queen, and they drove to the site of the new home of the Supreme Court of Canada. Their Majesties and the official party having taken their seats, the Prime Minister rose and said: 'May it please Your Majesty, I have the honour to invite Your Majesty to lay this corner-stone.'

The Queen rose and, accompanied by the King and the Prime Minister, walked towards the flag-draped granite block on which the corner-stone was to rest. There the Prime Minister handed her a special gold trowel. The huge corner-stone having been lowered into position from above by three white-overalled workmen, the Queen made the gesture of smoothing the mortar with the trowel and said: 'I hereby declare this stone to be well and truly laid.'

Then the Queen suggested that the workmen should be presented, and so she shook hands with two of them, and the King joined in the handshake and the chat. The third workman, standing ten feet above on a girder, was looking on, perplexed and nervous. But the Queen looked up at him, and that was as good as an invitation. Down the ladder he came and round the corner-stone, where the Queen gave him the hoped-for handshake, while the crowd roared with laughter and cheers.

Her Majesty moved forward to the microphone-desk and made the first speech of her life:

I am happy to lay the foundation-stone of a building devoted to the administration of justice in this great Dominion.

Perhaps it is not inappropriate that this task should be performed by a woman; for woman's position in civilized society has depended upon the growth of law. Canada is rightly proud of being a land governed by the rule of law. Her judiciary and the members of her legal profession have been true to the highest British traditions of Bench and Bar. It is fitting that on these heights above the Ottawa—surely one of the noblest situations in the world—you should add to the imposing group of buildings which house your Parliament and the executive branch of your government, a worthy home for your Supreme Court. Henceforth, on these riverside cliffs, there will stand in this beautiful capital a group of public buildings unsurpassed as a symbol of the free and democratic institutions which are our greatest heritage.

Au Canada, comme en Grande-Bretagne, la justice s'administre selon deux grandes législations différentes. Dans mon pays natal, en Ecosse, nous avons un droit basé sur le droit romain: il sort de la même source que votre droit civil dans votre vieille province de Québec. En Angleterre comme dans les autres provinces du Canada, le droit coutumier l'emporte. A Ottawa comme à Westminster, les deux sont administrés par la Cour suprême de Justice. Cela est, à mes yeux, d'un très heureux augure.

Voir vos deux grandes races, avec leurs législations, leurs croyances et leurs traditions, différentes, s'unir de plus en plus étroitement, a l'imitation de l'Angleterre et de l'Ecosse, par les liens de l'affection, du respect et d'un idéal commun: tel est mon désir le plus cher.

At the conclusion of this address, the Queen was given an ovation by the distinguished guests and the large audience surrounding the royal dais. Then Hon. E. Lapointe voiced the thanks of Canada to the Queen for her gracious act in laying the corner-stone. He said that the royal visit to the Dominion justified his hailing Her Majesty as the 'first Queen of Canada', while her 'compliment to the respect and love of justice predominating in this country will remain as an inspiring message'.

The ceremony over, the King and Queen walked with the Prime Minister to their waiting car. Amid cheers, Their Majesties departed for a drive through the city of Hull in the Province of Quebec, on the opposite side of the Ottawa River.

In Hull, it was a holiday, with the city's French-Canadian population increased by thousands of visitors from the surrounding district. Houses along the royal route were profusely decorated with banners and flags; and the streets were lined by the Régiment de Hull, the Hull veterans, the Ottawa Imperial Veterans, and several units of city cadets. During the whole procession, cheers welcomed the King and Queen, mingled with cries of 'Vive le Roi! Vive la Reine!' There was but one stop during the drive. In front of the Normal School, a group of girls dressed in white threw flowers at the royal car, and one girl ran forward with a bouquet of roses. The King told the chauffeur to stop, and the Queen, on receiving the armful of roses, waved her thanks to the delighted students, who cheered enthusiastically. Then the royal procession resumed its drive amidst continuous cheering, and crossing the Alexandra Bridge, returned to Government House.

Following probably one of their busiest mornings, Their Majesties were thoughtfully provided with a quiet interlude when they came to luncheon with the Prime Minister in the restful atmosphere of Laurier House. The house was decorated with irises and tulips, rose-trees and hydrangeas. In the dining-room, pink roses adorned the table. Shortly after three o'clock, Their Majesties left Laurier House, being escorted to their car by the Prime Minister and his sister, while the crowd lustily cheered the Sovereigns.

Instead of returning to Government House, the Sovereigns decided to grant themselves some relaxation by indulging in a drive in the beautiful countryside. On leaving Laurier House, the royal automobile crossed the Ottawa River and took the Aylmer Road. Near the Glenlea Golf Club, eight miles from Ottawa, after leaving its motor-cycle escort, the royal car turned into a tree-shaded side-road and stopped. The King and Queen quickly stepped out and strolled up the road bordered by half-wild, half-cultivated fields. They fully enjoyed the Quebec countryside, so picturesque with its luxuriant vegetation and its fine oaks, elms, and maples set against the blue hills of the

Gatineau in the background. The Queen picked dog-tooth violets. They trod over soft spring grass, crossed ditches, talked to farmers, and allowed themselves to be photographed. For half an hour they enjoyed to the full relaxation and scenery and the exercise in the open air. Then they re-entered their car and drove back, stopping on the way at Dow's Lake, a widening of the Rideau Canal. Here they met a boy fishing, who did not recognize Their Majesties. When he was told that they were the King and Queen he was so excited that he ran for home as fast as he could. Then the royal car drove on to Government House, Their Majesties arriving about four o'clock, refreshed and smiling, just in time for the Royal Garden Party given by the Governor General and the Lady Tweedsmuir in the spacious grounds of Government House as a celebration of the King's forty-fourth birthday.

In the evening the King and Queen honoured the Government of Canada with their presence at a royal parliamentary dinner in the ball-room of the Chateau Laurier. Driving along streets lined with troops and between deep rows of cheering spectators, the Sovereigns reached the hotel about eight o'clock. They were greeted by the Prime Minister and Mrs. Crerar, wife of the senior Cabinet Minister, who was acting as official hostess. The royal party proceeded to the drawing-room, where the Governor General and the Lady Tweedsmuir were waiting with members of the royal party.

Shortly after the toasts to Their Majesties, the Prime Minister rose and announced that, in spite of the crowded programme ahead, the King had graciously expressed his wish that the men and women who are the representatives of the people be presented to Their Majesties. This announcement was warmly applauded. A moment later, the equerry-in-waiting having come to His Majesty's chair, the King and Queen left the room, accompanied by the Prime Minister.

Earlier in the day, a notice had been given out that the Sovereigns would appear on the balcony of the hotel. Expecting the royal appearance to take place before and not after dinner, men, women, and children began assembling on Connaught Place as early as six o'clock. By half past seven they formed a solid mass of humanity, who cheered wildly when the royal car halted at the reception entrance on Mackenzie Avenue. After a long while they began shouting: 'We want the King! We want the Queen!' The shouts were heard inside, and officials sent a message to the Prime Minister, who apprised the King of the situation. Instantly with heartfelt graciousness the King expressed his desire to appear on the balcony as soon as convenient.

Fifteen minutes later, accompanied by Lord and the Lady Tweedsmuir and the Prime Minister, Their Majesties stepped out onto the flood-lit balcony, the King holding the Queen's hand. A rousing cheer rose from the enthusiastic crowd for more than four minutes when the Sovereigns re-entered the hotel.

Then Their Majesties returned to the drawing-room, where the dinner guests were presented. The presentation was followed by a little impromptu ceremony when Canada offered Their Majesties personal souvenirs of their Canadian tour. First, the Prime Minister mentioned that the golden bowl decorating the royal table was a gift from the Dominion to its Sovereigns. Then the Postmaster General, the Honourable Norman McLarty, presented to His Majesty a beautifully-bound book of purple morocco, containing the series of three hundred stamps of Canada issued since Confederation, as well as complete information about each stamp. The King, who inherited from his father, King George V, the world's finest stamp collection, highly prized the gift, remarking that it included stamps he had not seen before. To the Queen, the Postmaster General presented a large silver tray, on which were engraved in relief the three special stamps commemorating the royal visit. Smaller trays with a book of stamps were also presented to be given to the two Princesses, Elizabeth and Margaret Rose. The Queen expressed great delight with these gifts for herself and her daughters. The ceremony terminated with the presentation to Their Majesties by the Honourable Charles A. Dunning, Minister of Finance, of a case containing specimens of the silver dollar and the silver and bronze medallions, all specially struck to commemorate the visit of the Sovereigns.

From the drawing-room, Their Majesties were to proceed to Nepean Point, overlooking the Ottawa River, to view a display of fireworks on Parliament Hill. Because of the slight rain falling, however, they witnessed from a window in the Chateau the most splendid fireworks ever seen in the capital, concluding with the showing of huge likenesses of the King and Queen in a blaze of brilliant colours. From many vantage-points, scores of thousands of citizens enjoyed the magnificent spectacle.

Shortly before eleven o'clock, escorted to their car by the Prime Minister, the King and Queen left the Chateau. On hearing the noise of the motor-cycle escort, the throngs massed in Major Hill Park rushed to the road and lined up, cheering Their Majesties on their way to Government House, while from the Peace Tower carillon the strains of 'God Save the King' came floating on the air.

OTTAWA

THIRD DAY

SUNDAY, MAY 21, Their Majesties' last day in Ottawa, opened in the happiest way: the King and Queen talked for fifteen minutes with their daughters Elizabeth and Margaret Rose. The little Princesses were thoroughly excited and happy. Elizabeth, who took the receiver first, cried delightedly, 'Hullo, Mummy, this is *me!*' She assured her mother that she was 'looking after Margaret', as she had promised at Portsmouth. Margaret burst out with the news that she had passed her Girl Guides tracking test. The King spoke to his daughters, telling them to be good as usual.

The unveiling of Canada's National War Memorial by His Majesty proved to be the most impressive ceremony of the royal visit. At 10:40 Their Majesties, attended by one equerry, left Government House, and, accompanied by a mounted escort of the Royal Canadian Dragoons, drove amidst dense and cheering crowds by way of Sussex Street, King Edward Avenue, and Rideau Street. On their reaching that last thoroughfare, a fanfare of trumpets of the R.C.A.F., followed by a roll of drums, announced the approach of the royal cortège. Again a fanfare; and soon the open car rolled up to the crimson carpet opposite the royal stand, while a roar of cheers kept sweeping over the vast multitude.

As His Majesty stepped from the car, the Royal Standard was unfurled and the massed bands struck up 'God Save the King', while the King stood at attention. Then the bands played 'O Canada', and His Majesty remained at the salute. This royal recognition, following the precedent created by King Edward VIII at the Vimy Memorial on July 26, 1936, amounted virtually to the elevation of 'O Canada', with its beautiful music, to the status of the Dominion's national song.

Their Majesties were then greeted by Prime Minister Mackenzie King; the Minister of National Defence, Hon. Ian Mackenzie; and the Minister of Pensions and National Health, Hon. Charles G. Power. Then His Majesty inspected a guard of honour of one hundred veterans representative of all units in the Canadian corps.

The inspection over, the King and Queen mounted the steps to the base of the Memorial, and heads of the various national ex-servicemen's associations were presented to Their Majesties by the Minister of National Defence. Next, representing the bereaved mothers of Canada, Mrs. Catherine Lewis of Ottawa was presented by the Minister of Pensions. After this, the Minister of National Defence presented Messrs. Walter and Stanley March, designers of the Memorial.

The presentations being completed, Their Majesties, escorted by the Prime Minister and the Minister of National Defence and the Minister of Pensions, proceeded to the royal stand. Then the veterans' guard of honour opened its ranks and the pipers of the Cameron Highlanders marched and played the 'Lament for the Fallen'. After the last notes, the buglers sounded the Last Post. After a brief silence, Reveille was sounded. These moments were tense with emotion, hallowed by grief and gratitude, as the soul of the nation remembered and honoured her fallen sons.

After a brief period of silence, Prime Minister Mackenzie King advanced a few steps and said, 'Your Majesty, I have the honour to invite Your Majesty to unveil the National War Memorial.' On the Prime Minister's returning to his seat, His Majesty moved forward and gave the signal to unveil the Memorial, whereupon ten Grenadier Guards carrying their tall banners moved away from the face of the monument. Thus unveiled by the King, there appeared Canada's stately monument to the soldiers who had made for her the greatest sacrifice of all.

On the conclusion of the unveiling, the King spoke to the audience and, through a broadcast, to the whole Canadian nation:

> It is my privilege, as your King, to unveil today, in your capital city, the noble memorial to Canada's spirit and sacrifice in the Great War.
>
> It is almost a quarter of a century since the beginning of the Great War. Four years earlier my father had succeeded to the Throne. For many, the memories of the war will always have an immediate association with his reign. It has been given to me today to recall Canada's part in the great conflict. Fortunately, my task is already largely performed, for in the beautiful work of art which I have just unveiled, vivid and enduring expression has been given to the spirit of Canada.
>
> The time and the place of today's ceremony are not without significance. I am not surprised that it has taken many years to bring this memorial into being, and to give it this appropriate setting. On the battlefields of Europe, and throughout the Dominion, there are many memorials to Canada's honoured dead. Today, in her own capital, Canada dedicates her national memorial.
>
> The memorial speaks to the world of Canada's heart. Its symbolism

has been beautifully adapted to this great end. It has been well named 'The Response'. One sees at a glance the answer made by Canada when the world's peace was broken, and freedom threatened, in the fateful years of the Great War. It depicts the zeal with which this country entered the conflict.

But the symbolism of the memorial is even more profound. Something deeper than chivalry is portrayed. It is the spontaneous response of the nation's conscience. The very soul of the nation is here revealed.

Surmounting the arch, through which the armed forces of the nation are pressing forward, are the figures of Peace and Freedom. To win peace and to secure freedom, Canada's sons and daughters enrolled for service during the Great War. For the cause of peace and freedom sixty thousand Canadians gave their lives, and a still larger number suffered impairment of body or mind. This sacrifice the national memorial holds in remembrance for our own and succeeding generations.

This memorial, however, does more than commemorate a great event in the past. It has a message for all generations and for all countries—the message which called forth Canada's response. Not by chance do the crowning figures of Peace and Freedom appear side by side. Peace and freedom cannot long be separated. It is well that we have, in one of the world capitals, a visible reminder of so great a truth. Without freedom there can be no enduring peace, and without peace no enduring freedom.

After the King's address, the choir sang three verses of 'O God, our help in ages past'. Then His Majesty, accompanied by his equerry carrying a wreath, moved forward and, mounting the steps in front of the Memorial, placed his wreath at the base of the monument. Stepping back a few paces, the King stood for a brief moment, his head bowed in silent tribute to the dead soldiers of Canada.

His Majesty having returned to the royal stand, the Minister of National Defence stepped out and placed a wreath at the foot of the Memorial.

Now took place a departure from ceremony. Instead of returning to Government House according to schedule, the King intimated that he would pass along the ranks of the veterans round the Memorial. Once the service was over, Their Majesties, escorted by Lord and the Lady Tweedsmuir, walked round the pavilion and shook hands with veterans on all sides of the Memorial.

Their Majesties' mingling with the veterans lasted close to forty minutes. Then the King and Queen departed, standing up in the royal automobile and waving a reluctant farewell to a multitude shouting a continuous acclaim.

On returning to Government House from this popular triumph, King George and Queen Elizabeth planted two maple trees in front of the vice-regal residence.

At one o'clock, Their Majesties lunched privately at Government House with the Governor General and the Lady Tweedsmuir and members of the royal party and the viceregal staff. At 2:20 they bade farewell to their Canadian residence of Rideau Hall, and drove to Union Station. Accompanied by Lord and the Lady Tweedsmuir, Their Majesties moved through the station to the train, where the Prime Minister welcomed them. Standing on the observation platform, the Sovereigns kept waving until the train reached the end of the station platform, while as a last farewell from the capital a twenty-one-gun salute boomed loudly in the distance.

Before leaving the capital the King, ever mindful to meet as many of his Canadian subjects as possible, issued a thoughtful royal command: whenever Their Majesties stopped at a hotel, even for as short a time as half an hour, arrangements must be made to permit the King and Queen to appear on the hotel balcony, if the hotel had a suitable one. Indeed, balconies meant an opportunity for more people to see their Sovereigns. The King is reported to have made the significant remark: 'The more balconies, the better.'

The train stopped at Côteau Junction, where thousands crowded the available space, shouting a hearty welcome to the Sovereigns on the observation platform. As a little girl poised her box camera, the Queen touched the King's arm and they posed for her. The little girl cried, 'Merci', and the Queen said 'Bonjour'.

At Kingston seventy-five thousand persons—three times the population of the city—had gathered. When Their Majesties had stepped down to the red-carpeted platform, Prime Minister King presented the Mayor and Mrs. Stewart, from whom the Queen accepted a bouquet of mauve orchids. In the failing light of a beautiful day, during an eight-mile drive, Kingston extended a warm and hearty welcome to the Sovereigns.

In front of the City Hall were grouped civic representatives from many surrounding communities. From there the car proceeded to the Royal Military College, the only point where Their Majesties left their car. On the great quadrangle, the battalion of two hundred gentlemen cadets were drawn up in their crimson coats and white helmets. After his own presentation, Commandant H. D. G. Crerar presented to Their Majesties the senior staff officers. Then the King inspected the battalion, after which the staff of the college and their families were presented to the Queen.

Amidst rows of shouting spectators under the glare of street lights, Their Majesties sped back to the station. They mounted to the observation platform, and a cheer was raised by the onlookers as the train pulled out.

TORONTO

MAY 22 WAS TORONTO'S DAY. On schedule, the royal train rolled to a stop at North Station, which was draped with flags. Prime Minister King presented to Their Majesties the Lieutenant-Governor of Ontario and Mrs. Matthews, the Premier of Ontario and Mrs. Hepburn, and the Mayor of Toronto and Mrs. Day, while a royal salute was being fired by the 21st Medium Battery, R.C.A. The King having inspected the guard of honour, Their Majesties drove directly to the City Hall. There they were greeted by the Mayor and Mrs. Day, and escorted up the red carpet to the reception platform, impressively decorated with an immense blue drapery bearing the arms of Canada in colour, and surmounted by a red and yellow canopy upholding a royal crown. As he passed, the King saluted the cenotaph at the foot of the steps. As the Sovereigns reached their chairs and faced the spectators, the incessant shouts reached an almost deafening climax, while the band struck up the National Anthem.

The Mayor then presented to the King an address of welcome and loyalty on behalf of the citizens of Toronto, as well as a copy of it engraved on a plaque of cloisonné enamel and chased gold. The Queen accepted a bouquet of flowers from the Mayor's young daughter, Mary Day. Then Mayor Day presented to Their Majesties the members of the City Council and their wives.

Their Majesties having re-entered their car, the royal procession moved slowly to the Legislative Building, along streets close-packed with half a million cheering people. Heralded by a fanfare of trumpets, it rolled up the broad crescent of Queen's Park to the Legislative Building, decked with flying pennants bearing the crosses of St. Andrew and St. George. At the foot of the red-carpeted, canopied steps, Premier Hepburn greeted the King and Queen, and the royal party walked into the building and proceeded to the Assembly Chamber, where one thousand persons were already gathered.

When Their Majesties had seated themselves, Premier Hepburn stepped forward and read an address of welcome on behalf of the Province of Ontario. His Majesty received an illuminated copy of the address and handed the Premier his written reply.

Then the Queen graciously accepted a bouquet of lilies of the valley which was presented by Mrs. Ian Strachan, wife of the Member of the Provincial Parliament for Toronto–St. George. Premier Hepburn then presented to Their Majesties eight Ontario holders of the Victoria Cross. This was no hurried ceremony, for the King and Queen chatted with every one of them for some time. As each name was announced, there was a round of applause. Sergeant Colin Baron was first presented, and then Private Thomas Holmer, Captain B. H. Geary, Major E. J. Holland, Lieutenant Walter Bayfield, Sergeant H. H. Robson, and Captain Charles Rutherford.

Next the Premier introduced to Their Majesties the members of the provincial Cabinet, the Speaker, and the Leader of the Opposition, and their wives. In his turn, the Speaker introduced the members of the Legislature and a few high officials, and their wives. Once the presentations were over, the Sovereigns left the Chamber and proceeded to the Lieutenant-Governor's quarters for a period of rest.

The major part of this period was spent in an unofficial meeting with the famous Dionne quintuplets, who had come by special train to Toronto from their home in Callander. The little girls, then five years old, were accompanied by their parents and Dr. A. R. Dafoe, the physician who had attended them since their birth. The five little girls lined up before the Sovereigns and made their curtsies. Then Cecile hastened over to the Queen and stood in front of Her Majesty, holding up her arms. The Queen knelt down, and Cecile put her arms round her neck and gave her a kiss. Instantly the other four rushed to the Queen, who gave them each a kiss. But Cecile thought the King was being forgotten; so she went to His Majesty and took hold of his hand. The King bent down and whispered something to her, at which they both laughed. Then each of the quintuplets presented to the Queen for the little Princesses a photograph of herself with her name scrawled in large letters. On her part, the Queen gave the quintuplets white woollen coats, gifts from the Princesses.

While the King remained at the Legislative Building, the Queen, accompanied by members of the royal party, proceeded to the near-by campus of the University of Toronto, there to present new Colours to the Toronto Scottish Regiment, of which she is Colonel-in-Chief. From the west-wing entrance Her Majesty walked across Queen's Park and the adjoining Univer-

sity grounds, jammed with thousands of spectators. As the Queen emerged
from the Tower arch onto the parade grounds, accompanied by Brigadier-
General R. O. Alexander and Colonel W. A. H. MacBrien, her personal
Standard was broken out from the flagstaff and she was saluted by a storm
of cheers from the multitude crowding the four sides of the square. There
the regiment stood in line with its drums piled in the centre and the new
Colours resting against them. The regiment gave the royal salute and the
pipe band played the National Anthem. Lieutenant-Colonel C. C. Thompson,
the Officer Commanding, advanced and saluted Her Majesty with the sword,
and the Queen inspected the regiment.

The inspection over, Her Majesty addressed the regiment:

Two years ago I was glad and proud to become your Colonel-in-Chief.
Today I am prouder still, now that I have seen my regiment on parade.

Ever since I landed at Quebec I have found many proofs of the ties
which unite Canada and my native Scotland.

In giving these Colours to you who are a Canadian Scottish regiment,
I like to think that these bonds may be even further strengthened, and I
am confident that to you and to those who come after, they will always
be a symbol of the loyalty and devotion to duty which marked the
services of this gallant regiment in the last war. I leave them with you
in the sure knowledge that their honour will be safe in your keeping, and
with the prayer that they may be an inspiration to you in the future and
a symbol of devoted service to your regiment, your country, and your King.

The ceremony ended, Her Majesty moved on to Hart House, where the
King had walked from the Legislative Building. At 1:15, Their Majesties
attended the official luncheon given in their honour by the Lieutenant-
Governor and the Executive Council of Ontario.

Following the luncheon, about 2:20, Their Majesties entered their limousine for a drive to Riverdale Park and thence to Woodbine Park. Through
streets close-packed with onlookers, Their Majesties drove in a triumphant
progress.

Along Winchester Drive, the motor-cycle escort of the royal procession
was replaced by a mounted detachment of the Governor General's Horse
Guards. Presently the royal car rolled into Riverdale Park, a vast oblong
bowl surrounded by green slopes forming a natural amphitheatre. There,
on the flats, had been gathered seventy-five thousand children from Toronto
and the neighbouring district, while one hundred thousand spectators spread
out on the green slopes. It was the largest assemblage yet seen. On Their
Majesties' appearance, the children on the plains and the adults on the slopes
broke into a tremendous acclaim.

With the King and Queen waving their hands, the royal car began slowly to wind its way through the serpentine lanes, devised so as to give every section of the children an opportunity of seeing the Sovereigns. It came to a stop by the central pavilion, when a Boy Scout unfurled the Royal Standard at the flagstaff and the band struck up the National Anthem. Then the royal procession curved its way back along the lanes of excited and shouting youngsters, the King and Queen standing up in the car until it moved out of Riverdale Park.

Led again by a motor-cycle escort, the royal couple resumed their drive to Woodbine Park for the running of the King's Plate. This is the most important racing event in Canada, being the oldest race in North America. It carries a $10,000 purse in addition to the King's fifty guineas, first provided by Queen Victoria in 1859.

On reaching Woodbine Park, about four o'clock, Their Majesties left their automobile and entered the state landau. Escorted by a detachment of the Royal Canadian Dragoons, they drove round the track while a record crowd of more than forty thousand acclaimed their presence. At the entrance to the members' stand, the Sovereigns were received by the President of the Ontario Jockey Club, Mr. A. E. Dyment, with Mrs. Dyment, and were escorted to the royal box, where the Lieutenant-Governor and Mrs. Matthews and the Prime Minister also took their places.

As the field came out for the King's Plate and paraded to the post, the King kept his binoculars most of the time on a splendid chestnut colt bearing the number 14. The barrier went up, and Their Majesties rose to their feet. Number 14 was already beating his way to the front, and the King asked Premier Hepburn, 'What horse is that?' 'Archworth, Sir.' The King's choice, Archworth, favourite by two to one, won easily by ten lengths.

Their Majesties now walked across the track to the judges' stand. The King presented to Archworth's owner, Mr. C. George McCullagh, the famous King's golden cup with the King's fifty guineas in a purple and gold velvet bag. Their Majesties left the Park in the royal landau, changing back to their limousine on Woodbine Avenue.

Through streets lined with rows of cheering spectators, the royal procession then returned to Queen's Park for a brief rest and a quiet tea, given by the Lieutenant-Governor and Mrs. Matthews in their official suite in the Legislative Building.

Shortly before six o'clock, Their Majesties entered their limousine for a last drive through the city. Streets were packed with spectators acclaiming them from beginning to end of the drive. On the way, the royal car stopped at Christie Street Military Hospital by command of the King, who wished to pay a visit to these most deserving of his subjects: the Great War veterans in hospital. In the yard, on bleachers on either side of the path, were seated more than three thousand veterans, overseas nurses, and Silver Cross mothers, while in front were assembled in wheel-chairs and hospital beds more than two hundred disabled ex-servicemen. Their Majesties walked slowly through the grounds, stopping now and again to speak to as many patients as they could. But Their Majesties also thought of the bed-patients in the wards who were unable to be present. To them they spoke over a microphone. First the King said to them: 'To the many patients of the hospital too ill to leave their beds, the Queen and I take the opportunity to wish you all a speedy recovery.' Then the Queen spoke the kind words of a woman's heart: 'I am so sorry so many of you are unable to be with us here; I want to send you my kindest thoughts and best wishes.'

From the hospital, the royal procession continued its drive through the western section of the city on its way to Union Station. As the King stepped out of the car, the band struck up the National Anthem, and the multitude took up the words in one great song that was in itself an expression of homage and farewell. His Majesty inspected the guard of honour of the Queen's Own Rifles, while the Toronto Field Battery fired a royal artillery salute.

Their Majesties were escorted to the train by the Lieutenant-Governor and Mrs. Matthews, the Premier and Mrs. Hepburn, and the Mayor and Mrs. Day. As the King and Queen stood on the observation platform, the train began to move and a last cheer went up; the King raised his arm high above his head, the Queen made that inimitable gracious wave of the hand, and Toronto's greatest day was over.

TORONTO–IGNACE

PULLING OUT OF TORONTO, the royal train was acclaimed by thousands and thousands, lining the tracks for miles. About ten o'clock, the train paused eight minutes for water at Carley, a small station in a picturesque setting. Along a green slope, five thousand people were assembled in the dancing light of three huge bonfires of pine stumps and the white haloes of car head-lights. As the train halted, they raised a tremendous shout, and presently the Sovereigns stepped to the observation platform. Then came a rush of the crowd to the rear end of the train. The Sovereigns shook hands with several ex-servicemen and engaged in conversation with onlookers, inquiring about the place, the bonfires, and the veterans. 'How do you like Canada, Sir?' queried a voice, and the King replied, 'I love it.'

Next morning, May 23, the royal train steamed through a region of rocky hills, heavily wooded with tall pines, north of Lakes Huron and Superior, through the great mineral field of Northern Ontario, a land of magnificent distances, as for miles no sign of habitation is to be seen. The first watering stop was White River, the coldest place in Canada, with a temperature of $-72°$ the previous winter. When the train moved in at half past ten, the temperature was at freezing-point and specks of the previous night's snow-fall still lay on the ground. Almost all of the four hundred White River men, women, and children were assembled. There was even a band. Instead of a simple appearance, Their Majesties, prompted by their desire for infor-mation and exercise, decided to alight from the train. 'Where's the Mayor?' asked an equerry. But not being an incorporated village, White River had no mayor. Instantly the reception committee elected one of themselves, George Freethy, Mayor of the place for the duration. Escorted by the temporary Mayor, the Sovereigns walked among the villagers to the welcome arch, where the Queen was presented with a small birch-bark canoe full of flowers. Their Majesties chatted freely with the veterans, teachers, and Indians, and posed for camera fans. They concluded their stop by going forward to examine the huge locomotive, weighing 432,000 pounds. When the train left at half past eleven, great farewell shouts were let loose.

Shortly after five o'clock, the blue train pulled into Port Arthur station. The King stepped down briskly from the train, while a royal salute was fired by the 18th Medium Battery, R.C.A. The Prime Minister presented to Their Majesties the Minister of Transport and Mrs. Howe, and the Mayor and Mrs. Cox. The Mayor handed an illuminated address of welcome to the King, and the Queen was presented with a bouquet. Mayor Cox then presented to Their Majesties the Port Arthur aldermen and civic officials and their wives.

Their Majesties then entered their limousine, and the royal party, which now included the Minister of Transport and Mrs. Howe, and the Mayor and Mrs. Cox, proceeded on the drive through the gaily decorated streets of Port Arthur, thronged with solid lines of cheering onlookers. Their Majesties enjoyed a fine view of Port Arthur and Fort William stretching along the shore of Lake Superior and rearing their towering grain elevators skywards.

On reaching the boundary of Port Arthur, King George and Queen Elizabeth alighted at a specially erected platform and were welcomed to the city of Fort William with the playing of the National Anthem. After the presentation of Mayor and Mrs. Ross to Their Majesties, the Mayor in turn presented to the Sovereigns civic dignitaries and prominent citizens. Then the Mayor drew the attention of the royal visitors to a small encampment of fifty Ojibways who had come about five hundred miles to pay homage to their 'Great White Father'. Both Sovereigns evinced a desire to visit the camp. They walked over to the birch-bark tepees which enclosed a great fire, over which hung blackened pots and kettles. They shook hands and chatted with Indian chiefs in full head-dress, spoke to squaws with plaited hair, and smiled at papooses in shoulder carriers. They also admired some specimens of Indian craftsmanship. The encampment being on the bank of the McIntyre River, eight braves gave an exhibition of their skill with two birch-bark canoes. As Their Majesties departed, the Ojibways went into a dance of joy, prancing and whooping in honour of the royal visitors.

The royal procession then re-formed and proceeded to Fort William station through streets lined with cheering citizens and visitors. On reaching the station about half past six, Their Majesties were saluted by the strains of the National Anthem; the King inspected a guard of honour composed of sixty-four veterans of the World War and the Boer War. Farewell cheers followed Their Majesties into the station, and presently the blue train pulled out for the West with the Sovereigns waving from the rear platform.

After leaving Fort William, the train passed into the Lake of the Woods country, so attractive with its numerous lakes and fine woodland. About ten o'clock, when the blue train drew to a stop at Ignace, a rural community of four hundred souls, the whole population, from old men to women with babes in arms, rushed to the royal coach. Soon Their Majesties appeared and were received with rounds of shouts. During a short silence, a little girl shrieked, 'Mummy, I want to see the King; you said I could if I was a good girl.' The King and Queen laughed heartily, and in no time the child was lifted up to the royal couple, who both shook hands with the undismayed youngster. A little later, seeing the number of children around the train, the Queen remarked laughingly to the local schoolmaster: 'Should not those children be in bed?' and the children yelled: 'Oh, no! We wanted to see the King!' Presently the train rolled off amidst joyful acclaim from every one, old and young, of the four hundred inhabitants of Ignace.

WINNIPEG

ABOUT EIGHT O'CLOCK, Wednesday morning, May 24, the royal train crossed from Ontario into Manitoba. The country gradually assumed a different aspect with its sparsely-wooded, flat land, the beginning of the prairies.

At Winnipeg a steady rain, which had started the night before, kept beating down during the whole morning. At half past ten the royal train pulled slowly into the bunting-draped depot, and Their Majesties descended to the platform. Prime Minister King presented to the Sovereigns the Lieutenant-Governor of Manitoba and Mrs. Tupper, Premier John Bracken and Mrs. Bracken, Mayor John Queen and his daughter, Mrs. Queen-Hughes.

As Their Majesties left the station by the west-end exit, they were greeted by tumultuous cheering, while a royal salute was fired by the C Battery, R.C.H.A., at Fort Osborne. The band played the National Anthem and the King inspected the guard of honour formed by the Winnipeg Grenadiers, of which His Majesty was Colonel-in-Chief.

When the royal automobile drew up, the Queen seemed disappointed to find that the top had been raised against the light drizzling rain that was still falling. 'Can they put that top down?' she asked the King, who glanced at the sky and remarked that there was no probable let-up in the rain. 'That is all right; I can carry an umbrella,' replied Her Majesty. The King spoke to his equerry, and the Mounted Police put down the top, while an outburst of cheers greeted the considerate gesture of the royal couple. An equerry brought an umbrella to the Queen, who remarked with a twinkle in her eye: 'I am so glad you found it; that's the only one we've got.'

Accompanied by a mounted escort of Lord Strathcona's Horse, resplendent in scarlet tunics and brass helmets, the royal procession moved on, the King, indifferent to the rain, saluting to right and left, while the Queen, holding her umbrella high above her hat, waved with her right hand. To a continuous wave of acclaiming shouts, the Sovereigns proceeded up Main Street to the City Hall. Mayor Queen and his younger daughter, Mrs. R. A. Wise, greeted Their Majesties and led them to the red-canopied platform bordering the street in front of the City Hall. The King and Queen signed the city register, and Her Majesty was presented with a bouquet of roses.

Their Majesties next drove to the Legislative Buildings through streets handsomely decorated and packed with thousands of dripping but cheering people. At the foot of the steps leading to the southern entrance of the Legislative Buildings, Their Majesties were received by the Premier and Mrs. Bracken. The ovation from the spectators thronging the grounds swelled to such a crescendo that the Sovereigns turned round and paused a moment, the King saluting and the Queen waving to the crowd.

After a ten-minute rest in the Lieutenant-Governor's reception room, Their Majesties emerged from the main entrance of the building and walked to the red-draped royal platform, greeted with the strains of the National Anthem.

Premier Bracken read an address of welcome on behalf of the citizens of Manitoba. After expressing the Province's deep loyalty to Their Majesties, he paid tribute to the French and British pioneers who, bringing westward the spirit of civilization and justice, wrested Manitoba from the wilderness.

To Manitoba's address the King handed a written reply in which he conveyed to its citizens his thanks for their kind sentiments and fine welcome, and added: 'The people of Manitoba, having united many races in a common citizenship, may well be proud that the practice of tolerance and democratic principles has borne such splendid fruit. By their energy and determination they have contributed in substantial measure to the building of this great

Dominion.' He ended by thanking the Province for its assurances of loyalty and expressing hope for its prosperity.

Leaving the reception platform, Their Majesties proceeded to the Legislative Chamber, already filled with official and special guests. The King and Queen stood at the foot of the throne, and Premier Bracken presented members of his Cabinet, the Speaker, and their wives. In turn the Speaker presented other officials. After signing the province's register, Their Majesties left the Legislative Building.

At quarter past one, from the library on the first floor of Government House, King George spoke to the Empire and the world, as follows:

> Today is Queen Victoria's birthday, as well as Empire Day, and I am glad that I can speak to you on this day amid surroundings eloquent of the Empire's achievement since Queen Victoria was born. Winnipeg, the city from which I am speaking, was no more than a fort and hamlet upon the open prairie when Queen Victoria began to rule. Today it is a monument to the faith and energy which have created and upheld the world-wide Empire of our time.
>
> The journey which the Queen and I are making in Canada has been a deeply moving experience, and I welcome this opportunity of sharing with my subjects in all parts of the world some of the thought and feeling which it has inspired in me.
>
> We often talk of the Old World and the New. It is one of the greatest services of the British Empire that it serves to link and harmonize the two. That part of the British realm which lies in Europe and in Asia looks back upon many centuries of civilized life and growth. That part of it which lies in America, and Africa, and the two great sister nations of Australia and New Zealand has made its place in world society within the last hundred years.
>
> For a long period in history it was the mind of Europe which led the march and fixed the aims of progress in the world. But that tide of inspiration is no longer running as it did in times gone by. The Christian civilization of Europe is now profoundly troubled and challenged from within. We are striving to restore its standards, though the task is long and hard. Asia too is changing fast, and its mind is deeply disturbed. Is not this a moment when the Old World in its turn might look for hope and guidance to the achievements of the New?
>
> There is one example in particular which North America can offer to other parts of the world. A century ago, when Queen Victoria began her reign, a great constitutional struggle was in progress in the Canadian provinces. But soon after this time the provinces of Canada achieved responsible self-government. Freedom and responsibility led them gradually to compose their differences and to cement this noble federation from sea to sea.

The sense of race may be a dangerous and disrupting force, but English and French have shown in Canada that they can keep the pride and distinctive culture which it inspires, while yet combining to establish a broader freedom and security than either could have achieved alone.

Nor is that the only chapter in North American history that deserves consideration. Canada and the United States have had to dispose of searching differences of aim and interest during the past hundred years; but never has one of those differences been resolved by force or by threat. No man, thank God, will ever again conceive of such arbitrament between the peoples of my Empire and the people of the United States. The faith in reason and fair play, which we share with them, is one of the chief ideals that guide the British Empire in all its ways today. It is not in power or wealth alone, not in dominion over other peoples, that the true greatness of an empire consists. Those things are but the instrument; they are not the end or the ideal. The end is freedom, justice, and peace in equal measure for all, secure against attack from without and from within.

It is only by adding to the spiritual dignity and material happiness of human life in all its myriad homes that an empire can claim to be of service to its own peoples and to the world.

I would end with a special word of greeting to those of my listeners who are young. It is true—and I deplore it deeply—that the skies are overcast in more than one quarter at the present time. Do not on that account lose heart. Life is a great adventure and every one of you can be a pioneer, blazing by thought and service a trail to better things.

Hold fast to all that is just and of good report in the heritage which your fathers have left to you, but strive also to improve and equalize that heritage for all men and women in the years to come. Remember, too, that the key to all true progress lies in faith, hope, and love. May God give you their support and may God help them to prevail.

At half past one Their Majesties walked down to the dining-room of Government House to attend the luncheon given in their honour by the Lieutenant-Governor and Mrs. Tupper. At the head table with Their Majesties were the Lieutenant-Governor and Mrs. Tupper, Prime Minister Mackenzie King, Premier Bracken, and Mrs. Bracken. In the course of the luncheon, the Queen plied the Premier with so many questions about agricultural conditions in the West that to indicate zones, boundaries, and business centres, Mr. Bracken made use of bread crumbs on the table, joining or dividing them by faint lines with a pencil on the table-cloth. Queen Elizabeth was keenly interested and said she regretted that she would have to leave the map behind.

At quarter past three, Their Majesties left Government House for a twenty-eight-mile tour of streets and parks through the city. As the royal car moved off, the sun came out, to the great delight of the people of Winnipeg. The most enthusiastic welcome was staged by school children in

Assiniboine Park. Streaming from rural Manitoba and representing over a hundred different schools, about fifteen thousand youngsters—including more than four thousand Girl Guides and Boy Scouts—were massed along the driveways. With excited faces, the children flapped their Union Jacks and shouted wildly when Their Majesties waved and smiled at them as their car rolled along the driveways.

From Assiniboine Park the procession made its way to Polo Park, where another contingent of eight thousand children was assembled. Their Majesties left their limousine and walked the length of the grandstand, while the band of a Minnesota high school played the National Anthem, and the youngsters, each waving a small flag, extended to the royal visitors an exuberant ovation.

The Sovereigns also went down a line of Indian chieftains, several in war paint and native costumes, representing the Cree, Ojibway, and Sioux tribes of Manitoba. One of them, Chief Kesik, was proudly displaying a Distinguished Conduct Medal of the Great War. Another, Chief Hotain, who had fought under Sitting Bull against American forces in 1876, unexpectedly offered a pipe of peace to His Majesty. The King accepted it and thanked the eighty-five-year-old warrior.

Next the Sovereigns crossed over to St. Boniface on the eastern bank of the Red River. As the royal procession crossed the Provencher Bridge into the French-Canadian city, a tumultuous acclaim, intermingled with cries of 'Vive le Roi! Vive la Reine!', welcomed Their Majesties, while the great bells of the cathedral pealed merrily in the sky.

Returning to Winnipeg, the royal party proceeded to Fort Garry Park, where stands the historic stone gate, sole remnant of the old trading-post of Fort Garry, erected in 1806 by the North West Company and rebuilt in 1822 by the Hudson's Bay Company. His Majesty came to the ancient gateway to receive the royal rent due under the terms of the charter whenever a reigning monarch visits the Company's territory.

On the arrival of Their Majesties a band struck up the National Anthem and four trumpeters of the Royal Winnipeg Rifles, dressed in the dark-green uniform of 1885, sounded a fanfare. Then the Hudson's Bay Company flag was lowered and the Royal Standard was unfurled above the old fort gate. Their Majesties and the royal party having ascended the platform, the 'High Steward' and the 'High Bailiff' in turn called: 'Patrick Ashley Cooper', and Patrick Ashley Cooper, the thirtieth and present Governor of the Company, stepped forward and read an address of welcome to the King. Then the High Steward asked: 'Are you ready and willing to render your suit and service in duty?' Whereupon Governor Cooper replied: 'Ready indeed, and we hereby tender to His Most Gracious Majesty two elk heads and two black beaver skins with the humble expression of our loyalty, love and affection, now and so long as we shall live.'

Then Governor Cooper knelt on one knee and presented the King with a beaver skin, which His Majesty accepted with a smile. The High Bailiff cried: 'Let every man depart and keep his day upon a new warning and so God save the King.' The High Steward proclaimed: 'God save King George the Sixth!' Thus the ceremony terminated, amidst a tumultuous sound of applause.

Manitoba and Winnipeg's official farewell was a brief ceremony. The King inspected the guard of honour provided by the Royal Canadian Naval Volunteer Reserve and the Royal Canadian Air Force, following which he walked to the Lord Strathcona's Horse detachment and thanked the Officer Commanding and his men for the fine escort they had provided during the day.

Their Majesties were accompanied to the royal coach by the Lieutenant-Governor and Mrs. Tupper, the Prime Minister, Premier and Mrs. Bracken, and Mayor John Queen. Presently, with the royal visitors standing on the observation platform, the train started, acclaimed by the vast assemblage crowding all vantage-points around the station.

WINNIPEG–REGINA

LEAVING WINNIPEG, the royal train rushed westward into the valley of the Assiniboine River. Steaming past stations crowded with groups of farmers, it came to its first halt at Portage la Prairie about half past eight. About fifteen thousand persons were occupying every foot of space on the station platform and grounds. Here the Queen played the part of official guest, as she was the first to descend from the coach. Greeted with an ovation, she was received by Mayor and Mrs. Ireland, and Reeve and Mrs. McCartney, and was presented with two bouquets. Presently she was joined by the King, who was warmly acclaimed, and they were formally welcomed by the civic and municipal authorities. His Majesty inspected the guard of honour of the Manitoba

Mounted Rifles. After a stay of twenty minutes, the Sovereigns returned to the observation platform, the crowd burst into the National Anthem, and the train slowly moved away.

At 10:10, the locomotive glided to a stop at Brandon. Prime Minister King was first to step down to the platform, to be received by Mayor Fred H. Young. Then the King and Queen descended from their coach amidst an avalanche of cheers. After the Prime Minister had presented Mayor and Mrs. Young, Their Majesties mounted the reception dais. The Mayor introduced to Their Majesties the aldermen and prominent citizens of Brandon and then presented the King with an address of welcome, and the Queen was asked to accept a bouquet of orchids and roses. Following the presentation, Their Majesties suggested a walk the length of the platform where behind the cordon of veterans were grouped children, nurses, war veterans, and old pioneers of the district. Coming down from the dais, the King said to the veterans: 'Better form your line on the other side so that the children can have a good view.' As a farewell, the vast multitude sang 'O Canada', while the royal couple stood on the flood-lit car platform waving to the throngs.

About three miles west of Broadview, Saskatchewan, the train stopped, at the request of Their Majesties, who were eager for some exercise and a whiff of fresh air. They enjoyed the beauty of the undulating wooded plain. The King led the way so swiftly that the Queen and the equerries were soon left behind. Fifteen minutes later, ringing its bell, the locomotive began to move ahead to pick up the walkers. The King was then far ahead. 'Let us run and catch him up,' said the Queen, and, followed by the party, she broke into a run for over a hundred yards, when she stopped to board the coach, smiling at the equerries panting and mopping their brows.

Greeted by the cheers of waiting groups at every station, the train sped towards Regina (once known as 'Pile o'Bones', from the heaps of buffalo bones waiting by the tracks for shipment as fertilizer). In spite of threatening rain, the city had put on its gayest gala dress. Just outside the station, a huge silver-painted archway from which floated purple and gold banners formed the gate of welcome. All the way along the route lamp-posts were draped in gold and purple, with their bases surrounded by huge wheat sheaves, while stores and houses were decorated with Union Jacks and multi-coloured bunting.

At the appointed time, the royal train slid into the station of Regina. The Prime Minister presented to Their Majesties the Lieutenant-Governor and Mrs. McNab, Premier W. J. Patterson and Mrs. Patterson, and Mayor A. C. Ellison and Mrs. Ellison. As Their Majesties moved out to the main entrance of the station, rousing cheers rent the air. A royal salute was fired by the

18th Field Battery, R.C.A., the guard of honour of the Regina Rifles Regiment presented arms, and the band struck up the National Anthem. At the close of inspection of the guard by the King, the royal automobile moved off, accompanied by an escort of the Royal Canadian Mounted Police.

When the royal car crossed South Railway Street, the crowd broke through the police lines and rushed forward behind the procession, towards the near-by City Hall, cheering all the while. At the City Hall Their Majesties were received by Mayor and Mrs. Ellison, and ascended the outside steps under a barrage of applause from the milling crowd. After the Queen had accepted a bouquet of orchids from Mrs. Ellison, the Mayor presented to Their Majesties the aldermen and officials of the city and their wives. The Sovereigns then returned to the entrance of the City Hall, and were again acclaimed by thunderous roars as they stood at the top of the steps and waved to the crowds in the street.

The royal automobile next drove to the Legislative Buildings, where Their Majesties were greeted by Premier and Mrs. Patterson amidst ovations of the large crowd occupying all the available space of the grounds. Stepping forward to the microphone, Premier Patterson read an address pledging the loyalty of the Province to His Majesty. In his reply, the King thanked the citizens of Saskatchewan for their 'assurances of loyalty and devotion to my throne and person' and their 'reference to the Queen', and said that he realized 'gratefully that the people of Saskatchewan, as a part of this great Dominion, are making a significant contribution to the welfare of the British Commonwealth of Nations. Achieving unity through a common Canadian citizenship, men of diverse races are here proving the advantages of a way of life based on mutual tolerance and democratic institutions.'

To great waves of cheers, the royal couple, accompanied by Premier Patterson, Prime Minister King, and federal Minister Gardiner, stepped down the red-carpeted stairs, and the royal party entered their cars for a tour of the city.

The crowning event of the day was staged at the Exhibition Grounds, where twenty-five thousand Saskatchewan rural school children had gathered, as well as five thousand adults. When the procession entered the main gates off Elphinstone Street, a wave of cheering rose from the massed rows of children and rolled onwards to all parts of the grounds. At the same time, on a platform facing the grandstand, Indians of four tribes—Assiniboine, Saulteaux, Cree, and Sioux—in feathered head-dress and beaded deerskin costumes chanted and danced to the weird beating of the tom-tom in a ceremonial that proclaimed the King a Pipe Chief. Holding tomahawks and calumets, they jumped up and down, tossing their long feathers back and forth with wild war-whoops. Simultaneously four brass bands were blaring to the skies. There were folk-singers in national costumes and blues singers in cowboy hats, as well as hot-dog stands and a corral of Indian ponies. The whole scene was enacted with a regular din of cheers, music, and shrieks, and a riot of colours and costumes, in the boisterous and exuberant style of the West, mixing a touch of rodeo with the enthusiastic greetings to royalty.

Then the royal procession resumed its tour through the city amidst continuous applause until about four o'clock, when it glided into the peace of the Mounted Police Barracks grounds, which were not open to the public. Their Majesties were received outside the Officers' Mess of the western headquarters of the R.C.M.P. by the Commissioner, Brigadier S. T. Wood, and the Assistant Commissioner, Colonel C. H. King. Inside the Mess, the officers and their wives were introduced to the Sovereigns and then a delightful tea was served to the royal guests and party. Being twenty minutes ahead of schedule, Their Majesties next enjoyed a tour of the Barracks and then entered their automobile so quietly that their entourage were not aware of their departure and only discovered a few minutes later that the King and Queen had left them behind. There was at once official consternation followed by a top-hatted dash for cars and a swift pursuit, which lasted ten minutes before the royal limousine was overtaken. Making its way along streets packed with cheering spectators, the royal procession ended at Union Station shortly after five o'clock, and Their Majesties returned to their residential coach for a rest.

While in the privacy of the guarded station, the Queen took snapshots of some Royal Canadian Mounted Police and some of the newspapermen watching from a station window. The King changed to a lounge suit, and with the Queen left the train and enjoyed a brisk walk along the railway track for a mile or more, discreetly followed only by the Mounted Police fifty paces behind.

At half past six, Their Majesties left the station to attend the state dinner given by the Lieutenant-Governor and Mrs. McNab. Through cheering crowds they proceeded to Government House, which was proudly flying the Royal Standard.

At 8:40 p.m., through brightly-lighted streets jammed with spectators, Their Majesties returned to the station, the crowd extending them a tumultuous farewell all the way. After a brief leave-taking, Their Majesties presented to Premier and Mrs. Patterson their autographed photographs.

Presently the train moved off with the King and Queen hand in hand on the observation platform, waving a last farewell to the shouting multitude that surrounded the railway station.

MOOSE JAW–CALGARY

PASSING THROUGH RURAL STATIONS thronged with cheering bystanders, the blue train steamed towards Moose Jaw, and rolled into the station there at 9:15 p.m. King George and Queen Elizabeth were greeted by Mayor and Mrs. Johnson. A drizzle of rain had just started, and the King wore a light top coat, while the Queen carried an umbrella. As he escorted Their Majesties out of the station, the Mayor remarked that it was unfortunate to get rain at that moment. 'Oh, we think you need it, and rest assured it won't mar our enjoyment of this visit,' was the royal reply.

Mayor Johnson presented His Majesty with an address of welcome, and Her Majesty accepted a bouquet of roses from Mrs. Johnson. The city aldermen and their wives were next introduced, and Their Majesties then stood for a minute acknowledging the ovation of the people.

In spite of the drizzle, that the people might have a better view the top of the royal limousine had been put down, by royal command, and the King remained hatless and the Queen closed her umbrella. With a mounted escort of Royal Canadian Mounted Police, the royal procession went north on Main Street, spectacular with lights and colours. All along the route the crowds, dripping but cheerful, roared shouts of acclaim. At Caribou Street, the procession wheeled round, retracing its steps to the station.

At the station Their Majesties, noticing a specially arranged truck containing a score of invalid men, women, and children from the hospitals, walked over and talked with them for a few minutes. Then, saluted by a last cheer from the crowd, the Sovereigns walked to their train. At 9:45 p.m., after the official leave-taking, the 'palace on wheels' pulled out of Moose Jaw.

The next morning, about nine o'clock, when the blue locomotive reached Maple Creek, the crowd gave such a mighty shout that the engineer slowed down, and the King, rising from the breakfast table, appeared on the observation platform just in time to wave to the cheering bystanders.

Soon the train entered the province of Alberta, where the first official reception was tendered about ten o'clock in Medicine Hat. The nine thousand residents of 'the Hat' had been joined by more than that number of visitors from all over the surrounding country. Even before the royal train halted, tumultuous shouting greeted the royal couple, who were already standing on the observation platform. Prime Minister King presented the federal and provincial members for Medicine Hat. Amidst a storm of cheers, Their Majesties moved down the platform to a raised stand. Here the Queen accepted a bouquet of roses offered by the citizens of Medicine Hat.

Descending from the reception stand, Their Majesties walked to the station platform, stopping frequently to chat with the people. They spoke to James Dempster, a veteran of the Zulu and Sudan wars, and several other ex-servicemen. They also talked with some old-timers, including William Cousins, eighty-three-year-old pioneer, who had arrived in Medicine Hat before the railroad and opened the town's first store in a tent in 1883.

As the Queen again stopped to shake hands with two officials, the King remarked with a smile, 'Now, dear, I don't want to hurry you, but the train is waiting.' The royal visitors having mounted to the observation platform, the train pulled out amidst a storm of shouting and flag-waving.

When Their Majesties stepped down from the train in Calgary, Prime Minister King presented Mayor Andrew Davison and Mrs. Davison, and a Victoria Cross holder, Brigadier-General G. R. Pearkes, while the guns of the artillery near by boomed a royal salute and a pipe band played the National Anthem. Then the royal party moved through the station to the street entrance. His Majesty inspected a composite guard of honour formed by the Calgary Highlanders and the Royal Canadian Air Force. Entering their automobile, Their Majesties stood up to acknowledge the cheers of the crowd. The royal party proceeded to the City Hall, accompanied by a mounted escort of the Lord Strathcona's Horse. The procession slowly wound its way through streets gay with decorations and packed with onlookers.

At the City Hall, Their Majesties walked into the Council Chamber bright with draperies and fragrant with flowers. Mayor Davison presented an engraved address of welcome to the King, who in turn handed to the Mayor a portrait of the Sovereigns. The Queen accepted from Mrs. Davison a bouquet of roses offered by the citizens of Calgary.

As Their Majesties emerged from the City Hall and entered their car for a tour of the city, they were saluted by continuous shouts. Along the route, lined by fifteen hundred officers and men of the three services, supplemented by two hundred and fifty veterans, cheers preceded, accompanied, and followed the royal party.

At Medwata Park, facing Ninth Avenue and the Calgary Stadium, the royal procession entered an Indian encampment and a cowboy's corral, as colourful and boisterous a scene as in the days of the Wild West. In a straight line, thirty giant tepees reared their top-crossed poles and gaudily coloured canvas skywards. They were the homes of some four hundred Indians—Bloods, Piegans, Blackfoot, Stoneys, and Sarcees. In a row in front of the tepees stood a group of painted warriors dressed in buckskin ornamented with beads or porcupine quills and topped by towering head-dresses of white and black eagle feathers. In front of the central tepee, surmounted by a large Union Jack, a gilt-framed picture of Queen Victoria stood on an easel, to recall the signing of the treaty, in September 1877, when the five tribes present swore allegiance to the 'Great White Mother'.

From the crowd came a chant of welcome sung in high-pitched notes to the rhythmic beat of tom-toms mingling with the strange yowls of medicine-men, while some braves shouted the tribal 'yip-yip' and performed a war-dance.

At the end of the encampment was a corral with cowboys and and cow-girls in their picturesque costumes—leather trousers, coloured shirts, and ten-gallon stetsons, riding broncos at full gallop. Near by could be seen two old-time 'chuck wagons' complete with outriders.

No official stop had been scheduled at Medwata Park, but the Indians and cowboys were fervently expecting it. Their hope was realized: the King's interest was aroused by the picturesque sight and weird noise of the Indian camp. As the royal limousine halted, Indian women ran forward and spread buffalo skins on the grass for Their Majesties to walk on, and the Indian whoops and tom-tom beating increased out of sheer delight and pride. The head chiefs were presented in turn, the tribal interpreter calling each warrior's name in his native tongue and interpreting it for the King. Head of all the chiefs in camp, the Blackfoot leader Duck Chief greeted the King with the native salute: 'Oke-napi-is-tsi-piki-ninan', which means, 'Hello, Friend and Great Father'. Then came the other chiefs: Shot-on-Both-Sides, of the Bloods; Yellow Horn, of the Piegans; Crow Child, of the Sarcees; and David Bear's Paw, of the Stoneys. Minor chiefs and squaws were also introduced. The King and Queen shook hands with each one.

During the presentation, the street crowd broke through the Mounted Police cordon, being stopped only a short distance from the royal party. The chiefs showed the Sovereigns the picture of Queen Victoria and their treaty medals. The Blackfoot medicine-man, White-Headed Chief, chanted a song of welcome. Two tiny children, Holy Spring and First, came forward to present the King with a beaded medicine bag to be used as a tobacco pouch, but they were so excited that they gave it to the Queen instead. Then Duck Chief presented to the King a pair of braided gauntlets.

After a stop of about fifteen minutes, the royal couple went back to their car, and the royal procession resumed its drive through the city, and on to the station.

In the station, the King said to the Mayor: 'We are delighted with your welcome in Calgary, and particularly with the reception given us by the Indians. It has been one of our most enjoyable days in Canada.' Mayor and Mrs. Davison having taken their leave, Their Majesties stood on the rear platform waving at the cheering crowd.

BANFF

F ROM CALGARY the train swung through the green Alberta foothills. The scenery assumed a sudden picturesque grandeur, as the locomotive, skirting the rushing, foaming waters of the Bow River, climbed into the Rocky Mountains, streaked and capped with snow and rearing their steep walls skywards.

At half past seven in the evening, the engine stopped at Banff, in Banff National Park, nestled in pine forests and framed by a circle of magnificent peaks. Following the presentation of Park Superintendent P. J. Jennings and Mrs. Jennings by Prime Minister King, Their Majesties walked through the station, cheered by onlookers and children from the district. With the happy mien of holiday-makers, the King and Queen drove through the small town to the Banff Springs Hotel in the midst of towering mountains.

The royal suite occupied the central part of the sixth floor. From its windows could be seen the vast panorama of wooded slopes and snow-laden peaks, while in the valley the Bow Falls rushed between the rugged edge of Mount Rundle and the steep wall of Tunnel Mountain.

Hotel officials greeted the King and Queen at the entrance and led them to their apartments. From that moment, the Sovereigns at their own wish were treated as private guests and left to their own fancy. After ten days of official receptions, public parades, and impromptu station appearances, the King and Queen, rejoicing over the heartfelt enthusiasm with which they had been greeted ever since they landed at Quebec, could all the better appreciate an interlude of rest and relaxation, peace and freedom in the beauty and comfort of Banff. Indeed, they were not half an hour in the hotel before they were on their way outdoors for a walk. They passed a Mounted Policeman who, seeing them unattended when the twilight was gathering, decided that he should escort them at a distance. The King turned and, with a smile, said: 'Would you mind not following? We are quite all right.' For about thirty minutes, delightfully alone, the King and Queen walked in the enchanting peace of the glorious evening setting, visiting the falls and golf course and enjoying the pine-scented air. They returned to the hotel and had dinner in their suite.

Next morning, Saturday, May 27, broke clear and crisp, with the sun bright and warm. After breakfast the King, in plaid jacket and grey trousers, and the Queen, in tweed sport coat and skirt, went for a stroll. At 10:45 they left with some members of the royal party for an excursion. Accompanied at their own request by Brigadier-General Panet, they motored five miles to a point whence they walked for fifty minutes. They then drove to a vantage-point commanding a fine view of the valley and the surrounding peaks. On the way back, the Sovereigns saw a mule-deer. A black bear was also spied, which did not escape the royal camera. (Throughout the tour the King from time to time took pictures of the scenery and animals encountered.) An amusing incident also marked the drive along the Tunnel Mountain Road. A group of little girls were gathering lady's slippers when the royal car approached; in an impulsive gesture, Barbara Wakelyn threw all the flowers into the car. For a moment the Queen was startled, but picking up the flowers she waved them at Barbara, now happy but still astonished at her own daring.

Soon after lunch, Their Majesties left, at the Queen's request, for a ride in a democrat (known locally as a 'shay'). Unearthed from a local stable, the black high-springed vehicle was slung over four red wheels and was drawn by two white horses. Their Majesties sat on seats overlaid with buffalo robes, with scarlet rugs over their knees. On this drive they were driven by a local expert, Jim Brewster, and escorted by Brigadier-General Panet. After tea at the hotel, they re-entered the buggy and visited a beaver dam, where they watched the animals swimming about and bringing to their lodges skilfully-cut branches. The Queen took away for the Princesses chips from trees that the beaver had cut down. On the way back, Their Majesties sighted several mountain goats and a few elk and moose. They returned to the hotel, having enjoyed every moment of the day, thanks to the freedom and picturesqueness of the place and the unobtrusive informality of the stop.

Their Majesties dined quietly with Lord Eldon and Lady Nunburnholme in a private dining-room adjoining the banquet room, where the Dominion Government was giving a dinner for the fifty newspaper correspondents, radio announcers, cameramen, and other passengers of the pilot train. After dinner, Their Majesties happened to walk along the corridor just as the newspapermen were coming out of the main dining-room. The Sovereigns said good evening to some correspondents whom they knew by sight and stopped to say a few words to them. Other correspondents soon gathered round the group, and the King and Queen indulged in an informal talk with the whole party. The King particularly enjoyed the chat.

On the following morning, Sunday, May 28, Their Majesties began the day by speaking over the telephone to the little Princesses again. Shortly before ten o'clock, Their Majesties departed from the hotel to attend divine service and thereafter to resume their journey westward. They left refreshed and delighted with their brief week-end rest and with the natural beauty of Banff.

At 10:40, headed by Their Majesties' car, the royal 'motorcade' left Banff for Lake Louise over a gravel road cut into the mountain sides. En route they spied in a swamp one of the rarest wild animals of Canada, an albino moose, feeding with a normally-coloured companion. The King took motion pictures of the animals.

After stopping for tea at the Chateau Lake Louise, overlooking the green-blue waters of that glacial lake, Their Majesties drove on to Field, where the royal train awaited them. At Field a crowd of over one thousand persons broke into cheers as the Sovereigns alighted from their automobile. Their Majesties walked round the motor-cars to see the war veterans, and the children broke the lines to get closer to the Sovereigns. Then the whole crowd sang the National Anthem, and the King and Queen waved to them from the train, which was soon speeding on its way.

At ten o'clock the train pulled into the flood-lit station of Kamloops, where the reception platform had been thoroughly sprayed with chemicals to keep away mosquitoes. Twelve thousand people were crowding the station and surrounding grounds. Greeted with waves of applause, the King and Queen moved down to the platform. Prime Minister King presented Mayor

C. E. Scanlan and Mrs. Scanlan. The Mayor conducted Their Majesties to the decorated stand and presented the members of the Kamloops City Council and their wives, as well as the Victoria Cross holder Captain E. B. Bellew. The Mayor handed His Majesty an address of welcome, and the Queen accepted a bouquet of roses and sweet peas from Mrs. Scanlan. Two Thompson Indian chiefs were also presented to Their Majesties. Strolling first among cheering school children, the King and Queen moved towards the veterans and shook hands with some of them. The King inspected the guard of honour of the Rocky Mountain Rangers, and the Sovereigns then returned to their coach.

An hour later, about half past eleven, the train made a five-minute halt for water at Savona, where a large crowd surrounded the rear coach. The Queen came out at the sound of cheering and then, with a smile, she went in to the King, who could be seen reading a book. He laid it aside and joined the Queen on the rear platform, amidst renewed cheers. Even at so late an hour, Their Majesties spoke to several persons, asking questions about the place. The train then steamed on westward.

VANCOUVER

K ING GEORGE AND QUEEN ELIZABETH arrived in Vancouver on Monday, May 29. Almost from the moment of their arrival, the skies, overcast all morning, began clearing to full sunshine.

The ocean port was teeming with excitement and colour. From daybreak on, people by the thousands had been taking up vantage-points; by nine o'clock the down-town streets were a jam of humanity. When the guns announced the arrival of the royal train at ten o'clock, half a million people thronged the thirty miles of the morning royal route.

Vancouver was resplendent with draperies and shields, flags, banners, and streamers. Distinctive floral arches dotted the route, the most remarkable one being the huge arch at the top of Burrard Street: yellow broom, red geraniums, poppies, and roses, on a cedar background. Beautiful and fragrant, the arch remained without rival during the whole tour.

As King George and Queen Elizabeth descended from their train, guns boomed a royal salute from Stanley Park. Mayor Lyle J. Telford, attired in the purple robes of office with the gold corporation chain, greeted the King and Queen. The King inspected a guard of honour formed by the Seaforth Highlanders of Canada, and then the band played the National Anthem.

Escorted by a mounted detachment of the city police, the royal car moved off, followed by official cars carrying the Prime Minister, the Mayor and Mrs. Telford, and the Minister of National Defence, Ian Mackenzie. Driving through streets close-packed with spectators acclaiming their passage, Their Majesties' car swept into the City Hall grounds. There the King and Queen were greeted by Mayor and Mrs. Telford. As the royal party entered the main hall, the Sergeant-at-arms presented to His Majesty the civic gold mace, which the King lightly touched, by this gesture restoring to the Mayor his civic authority (for all authority is automatically assumed by the Sovereign the moment he sets foot in any part of the Empire).

A sudden hush fell over the Council Chamber as the mace-bearer, preceding the royal guests, announced: 'Their Majesties, King George VI and Queen Elizabeth of Canada'. The royal party moved up to the dais, and Mayor Telford presented to Their Majesties seven holders of the Victoria Cross: Major Robert Shankland, Captain H. C. Beet, Lieutenant R. Hanna, Corporal C. W. Train, Private M. J. O'Rourke, all of Vancouver; Colonel C. W. Peck of Sidney, and Major J. McGregor of Powell River. Then the city aldermen and their wives and a few special guests were also introduced.

Then Their Majesties were led to the reception stand in front of the north entrance of the City Hall. Below rippled a sea of men and women, whose joyous acclaim continued until the King and Queen walked to the edge of the stand to acknowledge the greeting. Mayor Telford then presented to His Majesty an illuminated address of welcome on behalf of the citizens, pledging Vancouver's steadfast loyalty to the King. Mary Robertson presented to the Queen a bouquet of pink and mauve sweet peas. As a strong wind was shaking the child's bonnet, the Queen hastened to take the flowers and said: 'Better hold on to your hat.'—'I am,' stammered Mary, grasping at her bonnet.

Their Majesties left the platform for a tour of the city. Passing a group of veterans from the Shaughnessey Hospital on King Edward Avenue, King George directed the chauffeur to proceed to the hospital itself so that the Sovereigns could visit with the ex-servicemen who could not be moved out of the building. Breaking off from the rest of the procession, the royal limousine drove to the hospital, where the King and Queen shook hands and chatted with several patients.

Rejoining the procession, the royal car drove through the residential district. Amidst continuous cheering the Sovereigns were driven to the fine grounds of the University of British Columbia, and then to the new Hotel Vancouver, for the luncheon tendered by the city.

Following luncheon and a brief rest, Their Majesties set out about half past two on a second drive through the city. The royal car first traversed the streets of the working-class section, which were jammed with bystanders of all races shouting a full-hearted greeting. The procession then drove to the lookout of the British Pacific Properties, fifteen hundred feet above sea level. Their Majesties alighted to enjoy the beautiful sight of Vancouver proudly spreading along English Bay and Burrard Inlet. Indicating the points of interest, Mayor Telford remarked: 'You will have to go a long way to see a more beautiful sight.' The King replied: 'We have come a long way to see it. I have never seen anything like it.'

Then Their Majesties, with Mayor and Mrs. Telford, proceeded to the 'Guest Cottage', where they were greeted by Major P. A. Curry. Attended by a maid, the Queen poured tea. At one point the Queen remarked to Major Curry: 'If I wanted to buy a home here, could I do so?' 'By all means,' said Major Curry. After a pause, the Queen added: 'This seems to me the place to live.' After a twenty-minute stop the royal party resumed their tour, via Highland Drive, and returned to the city to board the steamer *Princess Marguerite* for the trip to Victoria.

Amidst farewell shouts, Their Majesties stepped from their car and the King inspected a double guard of honour of the Royal Canadian Air Force and the Royal Canadian Navy. After the Sovereigns entered the pier building, Mayor and Mrs. Telford took their leave. Their Majesties were greeted at the gangplank by Captain Clifford Fenton. According to naval etiquette, Captain Fenton proffered the command to the King, who, accepting, became the official commander during the voyage.

At five o'clock, the *Princess Marguerite* turned her bow into the stream, outward-bound, and a twenty-one-gun salute was fired from Stanley Park. Four grey destroyers, the *Fraser*, *Ottawa*, *Saint-Laurent*, and *Restigouche*, shot ahead to lead the royal ship. Along each side of her, eight Indian war canoes raced forward manned by braves stripped to the waist, driving deep into the water their red, white, and blue paddles. Behind them followed scores of small craft. Overhead, two flights of three Blackburn Sharks, after diving to a salute, kept circling over the royal yacht, while higher up three Hawker Hurricanes patrolled back and forth along the route until the ship had passed Point Grey. Between a double line of fishing-vessels and pleasure boats, beflagged and pennanted, the *Princess Marguerite* proudly steamed under the Royal Standard.

During the crossing, the King had a message telegraphed to the destroyers congratulating the officers and crews on their seamanship. As night began to fall, great bonfires at Port Angeles, Washington, lit up the American shore across the Strait of Juan de Fuca, sending their welcome from the United States to the British Sovereigns. Similar bonfires lighted the coast of Vancouver Island up to Victoria, which the ship reached at nine o'clock.

VICTORIA

VICTORIA EXTENDED to Their Majesties an evening welcome in a blaze of lights. As the royal yacht came abreast of Ten-Mile Point, beacon lights flared from every point of land, and rockets shot high into the sky. The beautiful harbour gleamed like a fairyland with myriads of lights, while buildings and streets were illuminated with lines of coloured bulbs.

When the royal yacht docked, the Lieutenant-Governor and Mrs. Hamber, the Premier and Mrs. Pattullo, the Mayor and Mrs. McGavin, went on board and were presented to Their Majesties by Prime Minister King.

When the King stepped ashore, guns boomed a royal salute from Work Point. After Captain Victor G. Brodeur, senior naval officer, had been presented by the Lieutenant-Governor, the King walked over to inspect a guard of honour of the Royal Canadian Navy while the Queen remained under the shelter of an umbrella. Their Majesties then entered their limousine, with the top down in spite of the rain, and the royal procession moved off along streets lined with troops and packed with acclaiming throngs, to Carey Castle, which is British Columbia's Government House. The King and Queen were now in residence in Victoria.

Next morning, Tuesday, May 30, under a glorious, warm sun, close to one hundred thousand people lined the fifteen-mile route of the royal parade. At ten o'clock, Their Majesties drove away from Government House, the royal procession comprising the Lieutenant-Governor and Mrs. Hamber,

Prime Minister King, Premier and Mrs. Pattullo, Mayor and Mrs. McGavin, Defence Minister Ian Mackenzie, and members of the royal suite. For the first and only time during the tour, Their Majesties were attended for the day by a Canadian aide-de-camp, Lieutenant-Colonel V. Urquhart, D.S.O., M.C. Lined by veterans, sailors, and soldiers, the streets were thronged with cheering spectators all the way to the City Hall. There the Sovereigns were greeted by Mayor and Mrs. McGavin. In the Council Chamber, which was fragrant with roses, carnations, and English hawthorn, the Mayor presented to Their Majesties the city aldermen and their wives and also the reeves of the adjoining municipalities of Oak Bay, Saanich, and Esquimalt, and their wives. The Mayor then presented to His Majesty an address of welcome from the citizens of Victoria, and Her Majesty accepted from Mrs. McGavin a bouquet of roses tied with a ribbon of Lyon tartan, the clan tartan of the Queen.

When the royal car reached the Parliament Buildings at half past ten, a storm of cheers arose from the multitude as Premier and Mrs. Pattullo greeted Their Majesties. After the band had played the National Anthem, the King inspected a guard of honour of the Fifth Regiment in their black uniforms and white helmets. Ascending the red-carpeted stairway, Their Majesties stood before the main entrance of the building, all hung with banners and draperies. There Premier Pattullo read to His Majesty an address of welcome on behalf of the people of British Columbia. His Majesty handed to the Premier the text of his reply, in which he returned his and the Queen's thanks for 'the warmth of the welcome we have received in this province'. After noting the 'rich and varied resources' of the province, he praised its present people, whose efforts, 'inspired by the courage and enterprise of those who came before them, have made an impressive contribution to this great Dominion and to the British Commonwealth of Nations'. The provincial Ministers and members and their wives, a Victoria Cross holder, Lieutenant-Commander R. Bourke, and several prominent citizens and their wives were next presented to Their Majesties.

This brief ceremony over, the royal party returned to their car for a drive through the city and suburban municipalities. Along streets thickly packed with throngs continuously applauding, the King and Queen passed, smiling and waving.

At Oak Bay, Their Majesties were welcomed at Cranmore Road by one thousand school children shouting, while the younger ones strewed tulips, peonies, and roses upon the road before the royal car, which drove between

rows of spectators. At the Municipal Hall, civic officials on a stand surrounded by war veterans greeted the royal visitors with cheers.

From Oak Bay the royal limousine re-entered Victoria City, through solid
rows of cheering Victorians, and drew up at 12:20 before the Empress Hotel.
About one o'clock the royal couple descended to the hotel rotunda, where
Premier Pattullo presented a number of prominent citizens. Their Majesties
then entered the dining-room, where two hundred and fifty guests were
already assembled.

His Majesty's brief address, which was broadcast around the world, aptly
summarized the royal feeling and thought after traversing Canada from sea
to sea.

The Queen and I have crossed Canada from east to west, from ocean to
ocean, and stand now on the shores of the Pacific.

Your kind words, Mr. Premier, have set the seal on the wonderful
welcome that has been given to us at every stage of our long westward
journey.

I thank you for them; and here, at Canada's western gateway, I thank
all those thousands of Canadians whom we have seen since we landed at
Quebec for the loyalty and affection that they have offered so generously
to us both.

To travel through so grand a country is a privilege to any man; but to
travel through it to the accompaniment of such an overwhelming testi-
mony of goodwill, from young and old alike, is an experience that has,
I believe, been granted to few people in this world.

We are deeply grateful for it; we shall never forget it; and the inspiration it has given us will hearten and encourage us for the rest of our lives.

In the course of this journey I have seen the old, settled parts of the
Dominion which have a long history behind them, and I have seen the
newer parts, of which the first settlement is still within the memory of
living man. When I remember that here I am as far from Ottawa as Ottawa
is from London, I realize something of the vastness of Canada. When I
saw the broad plains, changed by the pioneers to the uses of man, and
the mighty mountain ranges through which they cut their roads, I began
to understand the qualities of the Canadian people.

For most of you, the present task must be the development of the
heritage already secured by those who have gone before. Nevertheless, in
this vast land, you have also still before you the rewards of pioneering
and the prizes of exploration. You have only touched the fringes of the
great North. Once those northern wilds were considered of little value
except as the home of fur-bearing animals. Now they are being surveyed
and mapped, and settled so far as settlement is possible.

Valuable mines are being worked right up to the Arctic Circle. There
in the North is a field of enterprise for youth which it will take generations

to exhaust. I could only wish that it had been possible for me to make a trip into that region which holds so much of Canada's future.

Here, on the shores of the Pacific, I can realize the position which Canada occupies. Her Atlantic windows look to Europe, her Pacific windows to Asia and the Far East. As science reduces the barriers of space, this country will become a thoroughfare between two hemispheres. Some day the peoples of the world will come to realize that prosperity lies in co-operation and not in conflict. With the dawn of that brighter day, I look to Canada playing an increasingly important part in furthering friendly relations between the East and the West. With the widening of her role of international interpreter will come corresponding benefits to mankind.

About 2:30 Their Majesties left the hotel to go to Beacon Hill Park for the presentation of the King's Colour. Twenty-five thousand people acclaimed their arrival there. Their Majesties ascended the dais, escorted by Captain Victor G. Brodeur, senior naval officer commanding the Esquimalt base. The naval parade gave the royal salute with presented arms while the band played the National Anthem.

The ceremony was as beautiful as it was impressive, as for the first time in history a naval flag was consecrated in the presence of a British Sovereign. Facing the royal stand, the escort company formed a hollow square with the colour guard in front, while the colour party stood behind the piled drums on which rested the King's Colour, a white flag of silk with a broad red cross, bearing in the upper left-hand corner a Union Jack, and in the centre, the royal monogram 'G.R.' in gold, surmounted by a gold crown. On one side, in their ecclesiastical robes, stood Bishop R. H. E. Sexton of the Church of England, Bishop C. J. Cody of the Roman Catholic Church, and Reverend James Hood of the United Church of Canada, as well as two naval chaplains.

Stepping to the side of the drums, Reverend Mr. Hood recited a prayer for the King and Empire. Then Bishop Sexton moved forward and spoke:

To the service of God and the hallowing of His Holy Name, to the love of our King and Country, and to the welfare of mankind, to the maintenance of honour and the sanctity of man's plighted word, to the protection of all those who pass to and fro on their lawful occasions, to the preservation of order and good government

— We dedicate ourselves afresh — came the response of the seamen.

In continual remembrance of our solemn oath and in token of our resolve faithfully and truly to keep it to the end

— We dedicate our Colour — came the response.

The Bishop laid his right hand on the Colour, making the sign of the cross and consecrating it with the words:

> In the name of the Father and of the Son and of the Holy Spirit we do consecrate and set apart this Colour that it may be a sign of our duty towards our King and our Country in the sight of God.

Then the King moved forward, received the Colour from Captain Brodeur, and presented it to the colour officer kneeling on one knee, while the band played 'Rule, Britannia'. Then the King stepped back, saluted the Colour, and returned to the dais. The parade gave a royal salute, the Colour being dipped to the ground. Next the colour party marched and formed line between the two sections of the colour guard, and the band played the National Anthem. The King's Colour had now been presented to the Canadian Navy by His Majesty himself.

Leaving the dais, the King and Queen walked to the reviewing stand. The entire parade then formed up and marched past with drums beating and bayonets glittering in the sun, the Colour being dipped as it passed the King at the saluting point.

After the ceremony, instead of returning to Government House, the King walked over to the naval veterans' guard of honour and asked Captain Thrope-Double if he would line the men up in double file so that he could walk along the line. Then Their Majesties returned through cheering crowds to Government House, the remainder of the day being free from official engagements.

In front of the porch the Sovereigns found, drawn up and waiting, 'forty-five men of Angus'. All raised in the vicinity of Glamis Castle, they had been acting as an honorary guard during the royal stay at Government House. Appreciating the compliment of being guarded by neighbours of her childhood, the Queen reviewed the guard, giving each one a smile and a handshake, and then graciously consented to be photographed with the group.

About 4:15, three closed cars slipped away from Government House, carrying the King and Queen with the Lieutenant-Governor and Mrs. Hamber, Lady Nunburnholme, Commander Abel Smith, and two Scotland Yard men. Travelling by devious roads and leafy lanes, the royal sightseers enjoyed a drive through the countryside, beautiful at this time of the year with the red bloom of hawthorn bushes. The drive ended at Dunsmuir Castle, in Hatley Park, former home of lieutenant-governors.

Down the rhododendron-bordered and tree-lined driveway went the cars to the stone mansion, then unoccupied. On the lawn below the terrace, the royal party sat down to a regular basket picnic, with sandwiches and scones, and tea from thermos bottles. In front lay the blue waters of the Strait of Juan de Fuca, and along the seashore blossomed golden Scotch broom among green trees and shrubs. After tea, the King and Queen went for a long walk through the estate, visiting the Japanese garden displaying iris and wistaria, and the glen where a little stream runs through patches of wild flowers. At half past six the party left Hatley Park, reaching Government House shortly after seven.

At nine o'clock the spotlight at Government House was flashed on the Royal Standard to signify that Their Majesties were ready to watch the fireworks pageant to be staged from Beacon Hill Park, where twenty thousand onlookers had gathered. After a burst of aerial bombs, a message of welcome to Their Majesties was read over the radio, followed by music. Next a royal salute of twenty-one bombs illuminated the whole sky. Then the nine episodes of the pageant were fired, terminating with the figures of the King and Queen shining in the night.

At the same time, other rockets could be seen from Port Angeles across the Gulf of Georgia. It was the international salute of goodwill to the King and Queen from American citizens in Washington State. Fired from four ships of the United States Coast Guard, it was also the first welcome from the United States Government. The gesture marked a perfect culmination of the royal visit to Victoria.

VANCOUVER–JASPER

O N WEDNESDAY MORNING, the last day of May, the King and Queen breakfasted shortly after eight o'clock. A little later, Queen Elizabeth ordered gifts of flowers to be sent to the Royal Jubilee and St. Joseph's Hospitals, especially for the returned soldiers' wards. Promptly at 9:40 Their Majesties drove to the docks to start their journey back across the country.

On the docks were lined fifteen hundred ex-servicemen and overseas nursing sisters in uniform. After the inspection of the guard of honour of the Canadian Scottish Regiment, Their Majesties moved over to the veterans and were engulfed in the crowd of cheering ex-servicemen. They walked among them, chatting with them, shaking hands, and waving to those unable to reach the front ranks. When the Sovereigns reached the end of the line, the overseas nursing sisters rushed forward and surrounded the King and Queen, who shook hands with all of them. Finally Their Majesties entered the embarkation shed, shook hands with a century-old Fenian Raid veteran, and received the official farewells of the Lieutenant-Governor, Premier Pattullo, and Mayor McGavin.

After Captain H. E. Nedden, Commander of the *Prince Robert*, was presented to Their Majesties, the King and Queen walked up the gangway and soon appeared on the bridge deck. The royal yacht moved into the stream, and the crowd broke into 'Auld Lang Syne', while guns boomed from Work Point.

Escorted by four Canadian destroyers, the royal yacht now sped on her way to Vancouver. Delighted with the greenery of the many islands viewed from the bridge, the Queen remarked to Captain Nedden: 'I wish we could buy one of these islands.' 'Why buy them?' was the quick rejoinder; 'They are all yours now.'

Luncheon was served to Their Majesties in the observation room, so that they should miss no part of the scenery. The *Prince Robert* docked at Vancouver at ten minutes to two.

From the dock to the city limits clamorous throngs lined the route. From Kingsway the procession entered the Municipality of Burnaby, where more than thirty thousand spectators greeted the royal couple with cheers. From there the procession rolled into New Westminster, where over one hundred thousand jammed the royal route. The royal car slowly made its way into Queen's Park Stadium, where eleven thousand children raised a sustained cheer. The royal parade went on to the railway station, decorated with the Queen's colours, blue and gold. Here Mayor Fred J. Hume was to be presented by the Prime Minister, but Mackenzie King's car being delayed, the civic group found itself in the presence of Their Majesties without anyone to present them. So the Mayor, stepping forward, said: 'I am Mayor Hume, Your Majesties, and I am very pleased to welcome you to New Westminster.' The Mayor then presented His Majesty with an illuminated address of welcome, and Miss Dorothy Hume presented the Queen with a bouquet of orchids. After shaking hands with the invalid Mrs. Hume in her automobile, Their Majesties took their places on the observation platform of their coach as the band played the National Anthem.

Fifteen minutes out, the train halted at Port Mann to drop off its extra engine. More than one hundred veterans surrounded the royal coach, and Queen Elizabeth appeared in response to their cheers. 'Do you all live here?' asked the Queen. 'No,' came the reply, 'we come from all over the Fraser Valley.'—'It is very nice of you to come so far to see us,' smiled the Queen.

Her Majesty re-entered the coach, and when she returned presently, a voice asked, 'Could we see the King?'—'He will be here in a minute,' said the Queen. She chatted with the crowd, and soon the King stepped out and the crowd cheered him.

At 5:24 the train arrived at Chilliwack. Their Majesties walked down to the station platform, where Mayor and Mrs. Barber were presented by the Prime Minister. When the royal party moved to the civic stand, the bands played the National Anthem. The Mayor presented to the King an illuminated address, and the Queen accepted a bouquet of roses from Mrs. Barber. Following the presentation of the Reeve and aldermen of Chilliwack and their wives, the King and Queen mingled with the people, chatting and shaking hands with veterans, nursing sisters, and old pioneers. They then returned to their coach, and the train pulled out, while the onlookers cheered.

There were no more scheduled stops that night, but numerous people gathered at several stations simply to watch the passing of the royal train. A small band of dauntless ones were even keeping vigil at Chu Chua when the flood-lit streamliner rushed by about three o'clock.

The train pulled into Mount Robson station about 8:50, and Their Majesties alighted to get a full view of the towering dome of Mount Robson, rising twelve thousand feet. About thirty people had congregated in this lonely spot to greet the Sovereigns. Some had walked seventeen miles, and two had ridden fifty miles on horseback. The King and Queen exchanged a few words with the bystanders. In the group, a tiny tot started crying so querulously that the Queen could not bear it: she gathered the little one up in her arms and quieted it in a moment with gentle motherly soothings.

At eleven o'clock the train pulled into the village of Jasper, in Jasper National Park. After the Prime Minister had presented Major J. A. Wood, Jasper Park Superintendent, and Mrs. Wood, Their Majesties were welcomed by the Honourable J. A. MacKinnon, federal Minister for Alberta, and Mrs. MacKinnon. Then a large group of people from Jasper and surrounding mountain hamlets made the mountains echo with their cheers. This was time for the Queen to exclaim: 'Oh! the air here! so refreshing!'

The royal car then drove Their Majesties through the village, lined with members of the Canadian Legion, to Jasper Park Lodge, where they took occupancy of Outlook Cabin for a day. Situated on a point of land that juts into Lac Beauvert (whose waters vary from light green to deep blue according to light), the cabin overlooks the sloping valley and the encircling majestic mountains, with Mount Edith Cavell directly in front.

Half an hour after reaching their cabin, the King and Queen, accompanied by Major Wood, were on their way for a ten-mile trip to Maligne Canyon. At the summit of the drive, they left their car and walked down along the edge of the gorge, at the bottom of which a cascade still bores its way between two walls of rock. At the second bridge, the King wrote in pencil on one of the posts: 'King George VI, 1st June, 1939'. The royal couple also stopped at Maligne Lake. All the way, the Queen picked wild-flowers and the King took moving pictures, including some of a mule-deer and a mother bear and her cub.

At quarter past three, they left their cabin again, with Major Wood and members of the royal party, for an eighteen-mile drive to Mount Edith Cavell. They alighted from their car at the tea room not far from the foot of the Glacier of the Angels. The air was cool and bracing; the sun shone brightly. In high spirits, the King and Queen enjoyed the excursion with the abandon of holiday-makers. They called to each other, pointing out some curiosity. 'Look at this, Elizabeth,' the King would say, and the Queen would go over to look. They ran about and took photographs of each other. They walked to the edge of the glacier, and, when they were caught in a brief flurry of snow, seemed delighted to experience a sample of Canadian winter. 'Something we wanted,' said the King, 'but had not expected.'

Then the King with Major Wood climbed up to the plateau of the glacier, where, taking in the vast panorama of the valley and the neighbouring peaks, His Majesty remarked: 'Oh! the immensity of it all!' In the meantime, the Queen, who had stayed behind, collected coloured stones at the bottom of the ice, for the Princesses' rockery. On the drive back to the hotel, the Sovereigns had the car stopped and walked for two miles. When they were motoring again, the Queen said to Major Wood: 'Do not build any motor roads here. Do keep the natural beauty of the place.'

Back in the cabin at half past six, the King and Queen sat down for a cup of tea. They were alone when a knock was heard at the door. Queen Elizabeth opened it. 'Good evening, Mr. Glass,' she said; 'Come in.' In came Bill Glass, the gardener of Jasper Park Lodge, to whom Their Majesties had sent command to come to Outlook Cabin. For fifteen minutes the Queen, a flower enthusiast, talked with him about the wild-flowers of the Rockies and the flowers grown in the Park.

At 7:15 the Sovereigns were out once more, to see the beaver at work. They drove to a small unnamed lake close to Lake Edith, but the rodents refused to perform, except for one that kept gnawing away so industriously that the King remarked: 'He is surely making up for his brothers.'

On returning to Outlook Cabin a little after eight o'clock, Their Majesties dined with some members of their suite. But the day was not over. About half past nine, the King—a moving-picture enthusiast—began, with the help of the bell-boy captain, to splice films that he had taken during the tour and that had been developed and printed by the photographers on the pilot train. As soon as the work was completed, the film, over seven hundred feet long, was run through the projector. It proved to be quite good and interesting. So ended the royal day of rest!

Next morning, June 2, refreshed after their one-day holiday, Their Majesties left Jasper Park Lodge, with the King's wishful regret: 'Oh! if we could only stay here!' At the station, they were cheered by a crowd of several hundred. The King stepped over a low barrier to mingle and chat for a few minutes with some of the fifty veterans present. As the train pulled out, at half past nine, the King and Queen remained on the rear platform waving a farewell to Jasper.

EDMONTON

O UT OF JASPER the railway line, skirting the Athabaska River, afforded the royal passengers beautiful vistas of many peaks and lakes. At Entrance, the first pause for service about half past ten, a handful of residents from the tiny hamlet greeted the Sovereigns. Ten minutes later the train was halted on royal command, and the King and Queen, with members of their staff, took a two-mile stroll down the tracks. The King walked with A. E. Warren, Vice-President of the Canadian National Railways, discussing construction and details of Canadian locomotives. When their walk ended, a signal was given for the train to come ahead and pick up the royal party.

About half past three a terrific roar enveloped the royal flyer; the King and Queen hurried to the rear platform, and on their appearance the roar rolled along, as crowds massed on both sides of the track for over three miles kept on shouting, right up to the station in Edmonton. Probably two hundred thousand people had gathered in the city: several hundred had travelled five hundred miles from the Peace River district; miners had flown more than eight hundred miles from the northern hinterlands.

As the royal train glided to a halt, the King and Queen stepped down to the platform. A band played the National Anthem, while in the distance a royal salute was fired by the 61st Field Battery, R.C.A. Then Prime Minister King presented the Lieutenant-Governor and Mrs. Bowen, Premier and Mrs. Aberhart, federal Minister J. A. MacKinnon and Mrs. MacKinnon, and Mayor and Mrs. Fry. Next the King reviewed the guard of honour of the Edmonton Fusiliers.

Moving out of the station, the Sovereigns stepped into their limousine. Greeted by dense, cheering crowds, and preceded by a motor-cycle escort of red-coated Mounted Police, the procession started on a tour of the city, down 101st Street to Portage Avenue, where the royal visitors encountered something new and magnificent: a mass welcome of seventy thousand cheering, flag-waving people filling two continuous grandstands facing each other for a distance of two miles on either side of the vacant avenue. (As a reminder of the royal visit, the avenue's name was the same day changed to Kingsway.)

The royal limousine drove the length of Portage Avenue and then turned round and retraced its way back. Near the end of the avenue the Sovereigns were surprised to hear some weird singing to the tune of 'God Save the King'. It was a group of Cree Indians chanting to the beat of tom-toms a Cree version of the National Anthem. The procession halted, and the King and Queen stepped down on a buffalo robe in front of an encampment of twelve hundred Indians, who had congregated from several reservations, headed by chiefs and tribe leaders in Indian dress. Chief Joe Samson, who had met the King's father and mother at Calgary in 1901, was presented, as well as Chief Ermine Skin. Then six-year-old Rosie Samson, in white buckskin, offered to the King a gun case and to the Queen a bag and belt, all in buckskin profusely beaded.

The Sovereigns re-entered their car while the Indians launched again into their Cree version of the National Anthem. Then, the motor-cycle escort being replaced by a mounted detachment of the 19th Alberta Dragoons, the royal parade proceeded to the Legislative Building. In front of the imposing edifice hung with shields and immense draperies, a dense crowd acclaimed the Sovereigns, who alighted from their car just as the official host and hostess,

Premier and Mrs. Aberhart, came down the steps to greet Their Majesties and escort them to the broad landing where the royal party was grouped. The Premier read on behalf of the Province of Alberta a message assuring Their Majesties of its 'sincere and enduring loyalty'.

His Majesty, having received the address from Premier Aberhart, handed to him his reply in writing. The reply thanked the people of Alberta for their 'loyal address' and 'kind affectionate words of welcome'. It then expressed the assurance that 'blessed as they were with a rich and fertile soil and with an enterprising and courageous spirit', they would, in spite of difficulties, continue to 'make their full contribution to the strength and welfare of Canada, which is such an important member of the British Commonwealth of Nations'.

Mayor Fry next presented to His Majesty an illuminated address of welcome on behalf of the citizens of Edmonton.

The official welcome over, Premier Aberhart presented to Their Majesties seven Victoria Cross holders, citizens of Alberta: Brigadier-General G. R. Pearkes, Lieutenant-Colonel F. M. W. Harvey, Major Marcus Strachan, Sergeant A. Brereton, Sergeant R. L. Zengel, Private J. C. Kerr, and Private C. J. Kinrose. As each name was called, the crowd cheered.

Escorted by the Lieutenant-Governor and Mrs. Bowen, Their Majesties proceeded to the Lieutenant-Governor's quarters for a period of rest, during which tea was served to the Sovereigns and members of the royal suite. After tea, Their Majesties walked to the balcony overlooking the Legislative Building grounds, to wave to the cheering crowd below.

As Their Majesties descended the steps, Premier Aberhart drew the King's attention to Mrs. J. G. Pattison, widow of a Victoria Cross holder. Their Majesties shook hands and chatted with her for a few moments. Then the Queen, noticing an aged veteran with an array of medals, spoke to him and presented him to the King. This man, Sergeant-Major James McGregor, once a member of the Scots Guards, told the King simply: 'You have done a good job for the Empire, Sir.' Prime Minister King presented to the Sovereigns Joseph Haire, who had served during the Fenian raids seventy years before.

Then Their Majesties walked to their car to resume their drive through the city. Crossing the High Level Bridge, the procession rolled along avenues and streets gaily decorated and lined with cheering citizens. In front of the green lawns of the University Hospital the Sovereigns had their car halted, and walked between rows of cots and wheel-chairs occupied by disabled ex-servicemen, shaking hands and chatting with a number of them. They were about to get back into their limousine, and the Mounted Police escort had gone back to their motor-cycles, when a little crippled girl was carried up to the Queen and presented a bouquet to her. Then, spying the group of paralytic children in their beds lining the street, the Sovereigns strolled along the sidewalk with a word of cheer and a smile for every child.

Continuing its tour, the royal procession came to the cenotaph, around which special bleachers were occupied by disabled veterans, war widows, and families of militiamen and ex-servicemen. In front of the memorial stood two veterans with a wreath. The car slowed down, but as it was not feasible to halt the parade, the King waited until he returned to the station and then sent his equerry, Commander Abel Smith, who placed the wreath before the cenotaph in the name of His Majesty.

At the station, the King and Queen retired to their residential coach for a rest before attending the Government banquet. At 7:45 they left the station for the Macdonald Hotel, along streets still tightly packed with applauding spectators. At the hotel they were met by Premier and Mrs. Aberhart. Shortly after eight o'clock they entered the banquet hall, where two hundred guests were already in their places.

During the dinner the crowds outside the hotel increased until the police had to send out calls for help: two hundred Calgary Highlanders rushed to the scene and ropes were stretched around the hotel crescent in order to keep a passage clear for the royal drive to the station. The pressure against the front ranks was tremendous. Highlanders and police stood first with joined hands and then with locked arms to form a human chain against the surge of the crowd.

Shortly after half past nine, on the flag-draped and flood-lit balcony appeared the King and Queen. Acclaimed by fervent cheers, they stepped forward and waved again and again to the crowds. When, a little later, the Sovereigns came out and entered their limousine, they were acclaimed by the waiting multitude along the streets all the way to the station.

At the station the King reviewed the guard of honour of the Edmonton Regiment. Then Their Majesties extended a farewell handshake to their hosts, Lieutenant-Governor and Mrs. Bowen, Premier and Mrs. Aberhart, Mayor and Mrs. Fry, and Hon. and Mrs. MacKinnon. To the Chairman of the Reception Committee, Percy W. Abbott, the King said of the Portage Avenue mass welcome: 'It has made us very, very happy. It was a splendid sight.' The Queen added: 'I never saw anything like it before.' Their Majesties boarded the train, which slowly pulled away, the King and Queen standing on the rear platform smiling and waving.

EDMONTON–GUELPH

D EPARTING FROM EDMONTON about 10:10, the blue train, after a run of seven miles, rested for the night on a siding at Clover Bar.

The first service stop of the day occurred at nine o'clock, at Wainwright, where twelve thousand persons had converged. Veterans formed a guard of honour, and warm shouts welcomed Their Majesties. Mayor and Mrs. Middleman greeted the Sovereigns, and a bouquet was presented to the Queen.

At Artland, the first station across the boundary in Saskatchewan, some five thousand people were gathered. Three little girls presented the Queen with a bouquet of roses, and Reeve W. L. Berry greeted the Sovereigns, amidst long acclaim.

About eleven o'clock, at Unity, more than twenty thousand people lined the track on both sides for more than half a mile, some of them having camped there all night. Mayor Loughridge welcomed Their Majesties, and his daughter Eunice offered the Queen a bouquet of pink carnations. The Mayor then presented some prominent citizens and their wives, while the crowd kept cheering the Sovereigns.

The train next paused for service at Biggar, with twenty thousand people crowding the station grounds. The Honourable J. G. Gardiner, federal Minister for Saskatchewan, presented to Their Majesties Mayor and Mrs. Wright, whose daughter Mabel offered the Queen a bouquet of roses. The Sovereigns passed along the guard of honour formed by Boy Scouts and Girl Guides. Members of the Town Council were presented, and the King chatted with some ex-servicemen.

At 2:20 the blue train reached Saskatoon. Waves of cheering from the crowd filling the square opposite the station welcomed the Sovereigns. Prime Minister King presented Mayor and Mrs. Niderost, while in the distance a royal salute of artillery boomed, and a choir of seven hundred high school

67

girls sang the National Anthem. Lieutenant-Governor McNab and Honourable J. G. Gardiner welcomed Their Majesties back to Saskatchewan. After the King had reviewed a guard of honour of the Saskatoon Light Infantry, the royal party mounted a bunting-draped dais. Mayor Niderost asked His Majesty to accept an address of loyalty and welcome on behalf of the citizens of Saskatoon. The King in turn gave the Mayor an autographed picture of the Sovereigns. A bouquet of red roses was presented to Her Majesty. The Mayor introduced to Their Majesties a number of citizens prominent in federal and provincial fields, as well as civic officials and church dignitaries.

The presentation over, Their Majesties in their limousine started on an eleven-mile drive around the city, whose wide streets were gaily decorated with flags and bunting and lined with one hundred thousand spectators cheering the royal visitors. Along the University campus a mass of ten thousand children set up a storm of furious shouts when the royal car rolled slowly by.

On Pacific Avenue was a display, on both sides of the street, of the products of the province. First stood a large stack of sheaves of wheat and a miniature elevator letting down a continuous flow of threshed wheat. Next were trucks loaded with bags of flour and oats, and boxes of fresh-water fish and poultry, and then an exhibit of rough and dressed lumber, beside which stood a young girl dressed in rayon made from wood. Then came an assortment of furs, with mannequins wearing the finest models of stoles and coats, and then a number of enclosures containing horses, cows, hogs, and poultry. On the other side of the street were lined, in actual operation, all the agricultural machines: threshers, combines, and tractors.

Continuing its tour, the parade came to the Saskatoon Sanatorium, where the royal car slowed down to pass between two rows of patients in their cots. Farther along, the royal car passed an encampment of one thousand Sioux and Crees.

Returning to the station, Their Majesties signed the city register. Then the Sovereigns walked to the reserved stands, where they shook hands with four veterans of the Riel Rebellion of 1885, including Thomas Swain, a 104-year-old pioneer. Their Majesties then bade farewell to their hosts, and the train pulled out with the King and Queen waving to the crowds from the platform.

At the little town of Melville, which has a population of four thousand, forty thousand people had gathered from all the surrounding districts within a radius of one hundred miles. The Town Administrator presented to His

Majesty an illuminated address of welcome on behalf of north-eastern Saskatchewan, and Her Majesty accepted a bouquet of roses from Mrs. Lane. Then followed the presentation by Mr. Lane of fifty prominent citizens of the district, including the mayors of Yorkton, Kamsack, and Canora. At Melville the royal train spent the night, resuming its journey about half past five the next morning.

About seven o'clock it crossed the boundary into Manitoba, and about quarter to nine made its first service stop, at Rivers, where more than two thousand people from the countryside clustered round, cheering. But owing to the early hour, the curtains of the royal coach remained closed.

Shortly before ten o'clock, departing from its schedule by royal command, the train halted at Portage La Prairie, as King George and Queen Elizabeth had expressed a desire to attend church service that morning. In an open car, the Sovereigns drove past fifteen thousand cheering spectators, to the church. At the church steps the pastor, Rev. George W. Abernethy, a Dundee man, was presented to Their Majesties, whom he escorted to their pew.

The service over, the royal automobile started its return route to the station, where a large crowd gave the Sovereigns a rousing farewell.

Past stations with groups of cheering bystanders, the train sped towards Winnipeg. This second stop there had been arranged on the King's instruction to compensate for an unintentional disappointment caused to war veterans during the first visit, when the royal car did not stop at the Deer Lodge Hospital.

By noon, the time of the train's arrival, the tracks were lined with onlookers for several miles from the western limits of Winnipeg to Union Station. Within the station, Their Majesties were greeted by the Lieutenant-Governor of Manitoba and Mrs. Bowen, Premier and Mrs. Bracken, Mayor John Queen and Miss Flora Queen, and Honourable C. D. Howe, federal Minister of Transport. The royal party proceeded to the station rotunda, where one hundred and twenty-three war veterans from Deer Lodge Hospital had been transported.

After the presentation of the hospital's staff, before going round the circle of disabled veterans, the King said to Major Oliver: 'Please ask the men to sit down; they must be tired.' Then the King and Queen moved round the circle, shaking hands, speaking words of sympathy, or nodding and smiling. When the Queen spoke to Sergeant Fletcher, a veteran of the South African and the Great Wars, who was blind, she was so moved that she held his hand until the King came up, and placing his hand in the King's hand, she said: 'Here is your King.'

At the end of the circle of veterans, the Queen was presented with a bouquet of white roses by one of the nurses. The King and Queen called out to their veteran friends: 'Good-bye to you all', and bade farewell to their official hosts. Standing on the rear platform, the King and Queen were acclaimed by thousands of spectators lining the railway tracks, the Queen waving to them and the King taking pictures of the scene. For seven miles more, from Winnipeg to Transcona, the track was lined with onlookers shouting farewell to the royal couple, who stayed on the observation platform until the cheering line finally came to an end.

Speeding eastward, the royal flyer slowed down only at Elms, where seven hundred bystanders cheered the Queen on the observation platform. After passing Wade, in Ontario, King George and Queen Elizabeth had the train halted for a twenty-minute stroll along the sleepers with some members of the suite. Coming to Minake next, the King and Queen acknowledged from their car the acclamation of a large gathering.

About five o'clock the train paused for servicing at Redditt, where ten thousand people had congregated, from Kenora, Fort Frances, and the Rainy River district. Accorded an enthusiastic welcome by the vast assemblage, the Sovereigns were officially greeted by Robert Mullin, Chairman of the School District, who presented Mayor K. P. Williams of Kenora and a few prominent citizens. After the presentations, the Sovereigns moved down the platform and listened to a selection played by the Cecilia Jeffrey Indian School Band, composed entirely of boys and girls of Indian blood. Then they talked to five crippled veterans before returning to their coach amidst acclamations.

Resuming its journey, the train sped through stations with the usual cheering throngs, and Their Majesties appeared on the car platform at McIntosh, Quibel, and Niddric. At Millidge, while the crowd cheered, the Queen, seeing two women on the platform with babies in their arms, descended and chatted with the mothers. A few moments after she boarded the coach, a red-clad valet stepped down with an ornamented box of cookies, on which the Queen had written: 'For the babies'.

The day's programme concluded with a reception at Sioux Lookout, where King George and Queen Elizabeth were hailed by residents from Sioux Lookout, Dryden, Fort Frances, and the neighbouring district. Mayor J. L. Moran and Mrs. Moran were presented by the Prime Minister, and the royal party moved to the flood-lit reception stand amidst a storm of cheering.

There Mayor Moran introduced a few prominent citizens and the members of the Town Council. Next the Mayor presented to His Majesty an illuminated address of welcome, and eight-year-old Lou Rorke proffered to Her Majesty a bouquet of roses.

Leaving the reception stand, Their Majesties, accompanied by continuous cheering, strolled along the platform speaking to several persons. They walked into a group of war veterans with whom they chatted a few moments. On the Sovereigns' return to their coach, which was encircled by the war veterans, the massed bands played the National Anthem, in which at once the whole assemblage joined. The train pulled out at 8:47, with the King and Queen waving farewell to Sioux Lookout.

Monday, June 5, saw a succession of those scenes of loyalty so frequent during the royal tour, when people assembled at decorated stations at all hours just to look at the blue train steaming past. It was so at Armstrong, at two o'clock, at Nakina at five o'clock, and again at Longlac, shortly before six o'clock.

At the service stop of Hornepayne at 9:40, fifteen hundred persons were gathered. After a clamorous welcome, Their Majesties came out and were greeted by Reeve W. C. Quinn, who presented members of the Council and their wives. Yvonne Metcalf, chosen by vote of the school children, offered Her Majesty a bouquet of roses. Then the Sovereigns proceeded down the platform chatting with veterans and bystanders.

About half past eleven, at the hamlet of Fire River, a service point, the whole population of twelve persons stood by as the Sovereigns descended. The Queen asked a trapper: 'How cold is it in Fire River during winter?' —'Sixty-five below, and the snow, she's six feet deep,' came the reply. 'Good heavens!' said the King.

Then the King suggested a walk and, with the Queen, started off along the side of the track, accompanied by members of the royal suite. Thirty minutes later the train came along and picked them up.

At Capreol a crowd of five thousand welcomed the Sovereigns. Mayor J. E. Coyne and Mrs. Coyne greeted the King and Queen, and little Shirley Coyne offered Her Majesty a bouquet. Then Mayor Coyne presented the King with Capreol's address of welcome, which in its simple and moving words deserves to be quoted here:

> We cannot take the place of Canada's high officials and do as they have done in presenting Canada to you. We, the common people, shall be content to stand along your line of march and wave our flags and cheer our hearty cheers.

We are the mothers who will bring up the next generation of your Canadian people in loyalty to your throne and in love to your person.

We are the people who will do the fighting for you when next your crown needs to be defended. We are the men and women whose brain and brawn keep intact this, your Dominion.

We are the common people you have come to visit, and we bid you welcome.

Thanking the Mayor for 'this most lovely welcome', Their Majesties walked back to their coach to a storm of cheers, and the royal train was on its way once more.

Shortly after half past six, the blue train slid quietly to a halt at Sudbury Junction, where seven hundred citizens from Garson and Falconbridge had assembled. When Their Majesties alighted, waves of cheers broke loose. Prime Minister King presented the Mayor of Sudbury, W. J. Laforest, and the Mayor of Copper Cliff, E. A. Collins. Then the Sovereigns entered their limousine for a five-mile drive through the countryside to Sudbury, whose streets were draped with flags and banners and lined with militiamen, Highlanders, and veterans. Their Majesties drove through the main thoroughfare to Athletic Park for the civic reception, where seventeen thousand school children raised their voices in a tremendous cheer. On the dais the mayors of Sudbury and Copper Cliff greeted Their Majesties; Mayor Laforest presented to His Majesty two addresses of welcome, one in English and one in French, and Miss Laforest presented the Queen with a beautiful bouquet of wild orchids.

About 7:10 the Sovereigns drove out for a visit to the Frood Mine. On Their Majesties' reaching the mining property, Donald MacAskill, Vice-President and General Manager of International Nickel, and Mrs. MacAskill were presented. Going to the change house, the King donned the regular underground clothing: fawn raincoat with a belt, steel helmet, and thick cotton gloves. To the belt was attached a battery to feed the flash-lamp carried in the hand or fixed to the helmet. The Queen put on an oiled-silk raincoat and a helmet and carried a flashlight.

Walking to No. 3 Shaft, the Sovereigns entered one of the sixty-passenger cages used by the miners. At the given signal, the cage began its descent at a rate of fifteen hundred feet a minute—almost twenty miles an hour—and dropped to the 2,800-foot level, which is two thousand feet below sea level. Coming out of the cage, the royal party found themselves in the shaft station, a white, concrete room reminding one of a London tube station. Then, mounting cars used for taking the miners to their pits and drawn by a battery locomotive, the royal visitors were carried eighteen thousand feet to No. 1 drift, where two miners were breaking the ore body with pneumatic drills. They were told that this ore yields eleven different metals: nickel, copper, gold, silver, platinum, zelenium, telturium, palladium, rhodium, iridium, and ruthenium. Both the King and the Queen displayed a keen interest in the work, and the Queen picked up a number of shining samples to take home to Princesses Elizabeth and Margaret Rose. The sightseeing tour over, the Sovereigns returned to the surface and entered their car for the drive back to Sudbury Junction. At the station a crowd of three thousand people gave a rousing farewell to the King and Queen as they stood on the rear platform.

At 12:38, the train glided into South Parry station, where it rested for the night, and next morning, Tuesday, June 6, departed at 6:45 before the eyes of over a hundred onlookers.

At the village of Washago, by 8:50, thirty thousand excited citizens of the surrounding district were drawn up on both sides of the railway line. As soon as the locomotive came to a standstill for servicing, there was a rush to the rear coach. Presently Their Majesties came out on the observation platform, and acclaim surged so loud that Reeve Mamford Horne of Orillia Township could not express his message of welcome but simply shook hands with the Sovereigns, who leaned over the platform railing. Then eight-year-old Basil Hefinstal was lifted up to the platform and said: 'May it please Your Majesties, on behalf of the Washago school to accept this snapshot book for the Royal Princesses?' And he handed a wooden-bound book of pictures of Washago to the Queen, who smiled and said: 'Thank you very much.' Then the train moved off slowly between two lines of shouting people.

At Beaverton, about 9:45, twenty-five thousand spectators cheered as the King and Queen on the observation platform rode slowly past. At Zephyr, where the locomotive stopped for water about quarter past ten, four thousand people acclaimed the royal couple, while the King took movies of the scene.

At Vandorf, beside the assemblage of hundreds of spectators, the members of the North York Hunting Club in scarlet costumes rode alongside the right-of-way; the Queen took a picture of that scene. At Richmond Hill, the crowd cheered as the royal flyer slowly glided through the station, with Their Majesties waving from their coach. At Oriole the station was filled with enthusiastic bystanders while the members of the Eglinton Hunt Club in pink coats rode with the pack on the polo field, a spectacle on which the King turned his movie camera.

Shortly after, the train entered the suburbs of Toronto. From that point groups of people were congregated at railway crossings, and from East York

Township the cheering line became almost continuous up to the city station; the crowds were so vociferous that the King and Queen soon appeared on the observation platform. Between Prince Edward Viaduct and the Don Station the train had to slow down on account of the throngs along the right-of-way, and then, at Yonge Street, as the people had swarmed beside and even in front of it, the train had to stop. Finally, however, it crawled into the station.

When the train stopped at the station, the King and Queen stepped to the platform. In accordance with the programme there was no official ceremony of any kind. An aide to the Lieutenant-Governor presented to the Sovereigns Mrs. William Bachus of Toronto, who twenty years earlier had directed the servants' hospital at Buckingham Palace. Then Their Majesties walked back to the train, to remain on the rear platform waving to the cheering crowd while the train pulled out.

As it sped along, the royal flyer was cheered by large assemblages of people at Weston, Malton, Brampton, and Georgetown. At Limehouse the entire population of the village stood at the station. At Acton three thousand people acclaimed the royal coach, as did a large crowd at Rockwood, the last place before Guelph.

GUELPH–LONDON

GUELPH TENDERED a rousing ovation to the Sovereigns, as fifty thousand thronged both sides of the railway line as well as the reception grounds. The train halted at a raised stand near the entrance of Priory Park. When Their Majesties alighted, Prime Minister King presented Mayor and Mrs. Taylor. On the dais Mayor Taylor presented to His Majesty an illuminated address of welcome and loyalty from the citizens of Guelph, and three-year-old Helen Galt Mitchell, great-great-grand-daughter of the founder of the city, John Galt, the Scottish novelist, presented a bouquet of orchids to the Queen. Then the Mayor presented to Their Majesties a number of aldermen, Members of Parliament, and representatives of war veterans' organizations.

The presentations over, Their Majesties walked to an enclosure where sat a group of blind people, disabled war veterans, war mothers, and nursing sisters. Presently the Sovereigns mounted the car platform and, as the train moved slowly away, the multitude roared a tremendous farewell.

From the station west as far as Edinburgh Road Junction, a distance of a mile and a half, the track was lined by thousands of spectators, cheering the King and Queen on the observation platform. When the train stopped for water at the Junction, thirty thousand voices joined in a great chorus of welcome until the train departed.

Ten miles west of Guelph, at the station of Breslau, the royal locomotive slackened speed on sighting a crowd of more than eight thousand people, and the Queen appeared on the observation platform.

At three o'clock the royal flyer pulled into Kitchener, having passed between two deep rows of cheering spectators for over a mile until it reached the station grounds, where one hundred thousand persons from all over the countryside were packed. The Sovereigns having descended, the band played the National Anthem, the Royal Scots Fusiliers presented arms, and the Royal Standard was unfurled from the flagpole. After Prime Minister King had presented Mayor and Mrs. Gordon, the royal party moved onto the dais, where the Mayor, in his gold chain of office, presented to His Majesty an illuminated address of welcome.

Stepping down off the dais, the Sovereigns walked to the war veterans posted by the station platform and chatted with them. Then, after a last remark to Mayor Gordon, Their Majesties bade farewell to Kitchener from the observation platform, as the band played 'God Save the King', followed by endless cheers.

Forty minutes late, the royal flyer now raced at high speed almost up to Stratford station. This proved most unfortunate, as twenty thousand school children from Perth, Huron, and Bruce Counties lining the tracks for two miles within the city limits had hardly any chance to see the Sovereigns when they came to the rear platform. Their Majesties expressed deep regret that 'the children should have been disappointed'.

As Their Majesties alighted, an incessant cheering spread among the assemblage. Prime Minister King introduced to the Sovereigns Mayor Thomas Henry and Mrs. Henry. Their Majesties having mounted the stand, the Perth Regiment Band struck up the National Anthem, accompanied by the skirling pipes of the Lucknow Scottish, and the Perth Regiment's guard of honour gave the royal salute. Then Mayor Henry handed to the King an illuminated address of welcome from the citizens of Stratford. After Their Majesties had spoken to a group of disabled veterans, they remounted the rear platform of their coach, and the blue train pulled slowly away with the King and Queen waving to the thousands thronging the railway line up to the city limits.

At the watering-point at St. Mary's Junction the royal train was acclaimed by ten thousand people. The local bands played 'God Save the King' and 'O Canada', and then Queen Elizabeth appeared on the rear platform, followed by the King.

Some time after leaving St. Mary's Junction, the King was presented with a surprise gift. Postmaster General Norman McLarty asked His Majesty to accept a complete series of royal train postal covers, whose cancellation postmark represented the Royal Standard with the inscription 'Royal Train, Canada'. The King, a keen philatelist, had already been presented in Ottawa with a valuable set of Canadian stamps.

The train came to a halt for servicing at Chatham, about seven o'clock. Forty thousand people, from all over Kent County, were there to greet the royal couple. Unfortunately the train overshot the point where the members of the City Council and the County Council were waiting for the official presentation. By this time the enthusiasm of the spectators could not be restrained: they surged past the veterans' guard and shut off all approach to the royal coach by the councillors. But the veterans opened an avenue for the Mayor and Mrs. Zink, who were presented to Their Majesties on the observation platform, and the Queen accepted a bouquet of roses from Mrs. Zink.

A crippled Scottish girl, Miss Jean Murray, carried in her wheel-chair by war veterans, was lifted to the railing of the platform, and the Queen, leaning forward, took her hand and said a few words of comfort and sympathy. Then the train departed, with the royal couple waving farewell in response to a roar of acclaim.

During the day Windsor had been submerged under the steady influx of people from Essex County and from Detroit and surrounding states. By seven o'clock half a million people, the majority Americans, were cramming all possible vantage-points along the railway line and around the reception grounds.

There was more than mere curiosity behind this mass frontier-crossing: it also represented well-wishing neighbourliness as well as international good-will and friendship. Indeed, both were manifested in Detroit's official invitation to Their Majesties to visit that city, and the official message from the Senate and House of Representatives of Michigan inviting the British Sovereigns to extend their visit to that state. These gratifying sentiments were also conveyed in a message to the King and Queen from Governor L. D. Dickson of Michigan, expressing the sincere good wishes of the people of Michigan.

About 8:10, for a distance of two miles before reaching the city limits, the royal train passed between lines of shouting bystanders. At May Avenue, from forty thousand school children in special bleachers rose continuous waves of cheers. Across the river Detroit's brilliantly lighted skyscrapers reared their towering structures, while a huge electric sign flashed its glowing message: 'Detroit welcomes Their Majesties'.

The royal train drew to a standstill in the station ground, in front of which was the reception stand. The platform was flood-lit by batteries of lights which made the scene as bright as day. Over one hundred thousand people were assembled there.

Presently the Sovereigns descended to the platform. Prime Minister Mackenzie King, accompanied by Postmaster General McLarty, presented Mayor David Croll and Mrs. Croll, and a royal salute was fired by the Lambton Field Battery. The royal party then moved to the reception stand, where the Mayor presented to the King an illuminated address of welcome on behalf of the citizens of Windsor, and the Mayor's little daughter, Constance Croll, presented to the Queen a bouquet of flowers.

Next came the presentation of parliamentary representatives, civic controllers, aldermen, military officers, and heads of public bodies. These presentations over, His Majesty inquired if any Detroit officials were in the audience. When informed that Mayor Richard Reading was there, the King suggested that he be presented. The Mayor shook hands with the King and bowed to the Queen. The King said: 'I am so pleased you are here, Mr. Mayor, because I have an apology to make.'—'An apology for me?'—'Yes, I am so sorry we are unable to accept your kind invitation to visit Detroit. To be sure, it is only across the river, but our time is scarcely our own, and—well, you will understand.'

Meanwhile the Queen had whispered to Mayor Croll, and a few minutes later Mrs. Reading was on the platform being introduced to the King and Queen. After this meeting, the Sovereigns signed the new city visitors' book. Again breaking away from formality, the King and Queen descended the western steps of the stand and mingled with the Canadian war veterans and American Legionnaires. The King and Queen went slowly round the reception platform, shaking hands and chatting with nearly two score of people, most of them returned soldiers.

Having reached the east end of the stand, Their Majesties returned to the coach platform, and the crowd, bursting all police resistance, rushed to the royal car, while the veterans and bystanders sang 'Rule, Britannia'. There were cries of 'Speech, speech', and a dour Scots voice called: 'Aye, lad, say a word or two, just a word or two', which greatly amused the royal couple. The train began to move, and Their Majesties stood on the platform, being saluted by outbursts of cheering. For twenty minutes they passed along a hillside of tightly-packed humanity, from whom came tremendous acclaim.

Passing with groups of onlookers waiting in the night, the royal train sped eastward. About midnight it slipped quietly into London station for the night.

LONDON–NIAGARA FALLS

T HE NEXT MORNING, June 7, King George and Queen Elizabeth awoke in the city of London, which, almost trebling its seventy-five thousand population, had gathered to its streets a multitude of two hundred thousand citizens.

When at 9:50 the King and Queen walked out of their coach to the station platform, they were met by Mayor Allan Johnston and his mother, Mrs. Isabella Johnston, who were presented by Prime Minister King. The Mayor said to His Majesty: 'The people of London and Western Ontario welcome you to your City of London, Canada.' A royal salute was fired by the Fifty-fifth Field Battery, R.C.A. Then the King inspected a guard of honour of the Royal Canadian Regiment and returned to the dais for the presentation by Mayor Johnston of a number of citizens of London and adjacent consti-tuencies, beginning with the city aldermen and their wives. Premier Hepburn of Ontario, with Mrs. Hepburn, was also introduced. Then the Queen accepted a bouquet from four-year-old Mary Jane Kennedy, great-great-grand-daughter of London's first mayor.

The presentations over, Their Majesties took their seats in the royal auto-mobile and the royal parade proceeded along streets with crowds stretched in deep rows. In the midst of continuous cheers the royal car came to St.

James Street, where disabled veterans were gathered on a special stand. Although it was not on the programme, the King had the car stopped, and the Sovereigns alighted and unhurriedly passed down the line.

Resuming the four-mile drive, the royal automobile stopped in front of the City Hall. The City Clerk came to the car with the city visitors' book, which the King and Queen signed. Then the royal procession headed for the station.

As the royal train began to pull out, the Lambton Garrison and Sarnia Collegiate bands broke into the National Anthem, and the crowd wildly cheered the Sovereigns, who acknowledged the acclaim.

Less than half an hour out of London, the blue flyer slipped into Ingersoll, where the station grounds were jammed with twenty thousand spectators. As the royal train was brought to a standstill, a wave of acclamations swept over the crowd, while Their Majesties descended to the platform, and the band took up the strains of the National Anthem. Presented by the Prime Minister, Mayor A. A. Edwards and Mrs. Edwards greeted the Sovereigns. Her Majesty inquired of the Mayor whether Ingersoll had a hospital. On being told that it had, she said, 'I am so pleased, because I wish you would give the hospital these beautiful flowers.'

When the royal party had taken their places on the dais, Mayor Edwards presented to His Majesty an illuminated address of welcome, and the Queen accepted a bouquet of orchids from Mrs. Edwards. After the Mayor had presented to Their Majesties a number of prominent citizens of the district, the King and Queen descended from the dais and, amidst continuous cheers, walked along the line of ex-servicemen, chatting and shaking hands with the veterans until the time of the visit was over. The train pulled out of the station with the Sovereigns waving from their observation platform.

During the brief stop the Ingersoll people had placed on board the royal dining-car two twelve-pound cheeses, renowned among connoisseurs for its excellent quality.

Less than twenty minutes after leaving Ingersoll, Their Majesties were visiting the city of Woodstock and its eleven thousand citizens. In a large square next to the station, a compact assemblage of thirty-five thousand people raised a frantic applause when the Sovereigns were received by Mayor J. A. Lewis and Mrs. Lewis. Mayor Lewis presented to His Majesty an address of welcome and loyalty on behalf of the citizens of Woodstock. Then the King and Queen walked among the four hundred ex-servicemen and chatted several minutes with a number of them.

When taking leave, Mayor Lewis remarked that he hoped, as did everybody in Canada, that Their Majesties would pay another visit to the Dominion. The Queen replied: 'We have already found the way to Canada. We may find ourselves able to come back some day.' Upon which the King said: 'The people of Canada have been wonderful to us.' 'Yes,' added the Queen, 'everything has been so lovely.'

At 12:44, Their Majesties set foot in Brantford. In a colourful setting in the large station grounds, a vast multitude—fifty thousand people—hailed the King and Queen with exuberant acclaim, and the guns of the 69th Field Battery, R.C.A., boomed their royal salute. Presented by Prime Minister King, Mayor R. J. Waterous and Mrs. Waterous greeted the royal visitors and conducted them to the reception stand. A massed chorus accompanied by the band of the Canadian Legion sang the National Anthem and 'O Canada'.

Mayor Waterous presented to His Majesty an illuminated address expressing the welcome of Brantford. Then on behalf of the citizens he asked the Sovereigns to accept a silver desk telephone as a souvenir of their visit to the city that gave the telephone to the world. Three-year-old Nancy Waterous offered to the Queen a huge bouquet of yellow roses. The Mayor then presented to Their Majesties the city aldermen with their wives, as well as several Members of Parliament and of the Legislature, and other prominent citizens.

After Their Majesties had signed the city visitors' register, they were asked by Chief Councillor Frank to accept an address of welcome from the Six Nations Indians and to sign the Queen Anne Bible which was presented to the Chapel of the Mohawks in 1712. With Chief Councillor Miller and his wife, Chiefs White Cloud, Blue Eyes, Black Cloud, and Little Bear were also presented.

Leaving the dais, Their Majesties paused along the walk to speak and shake hands with a number of ex-servicemen. Then, to the accompaniment of resounding acclamations, the Sovereigns stood on the coach platform until the train was out of the city limits.

From Brantford the royal train sped to Hamilton, where over two hundred thousand exultant spectators crowded thoroughfares ablaze with festive decorations. Alighting from the coach, the royal visitors were welcomed by Mayor William Morrison and Mrs. Morrison, who had been previously presented by the Prime Minister, as a royal salute by the 11th Hamilton Field Battery, R.C.A., roared in the distance.

Passing out of the station, Their Majesties were greeted with tremendous cheers from a crowd of ten thousand bystanders as the military band struck up the National Anthem. The King then reviewed the guard of honour of the Royal Hamilton Light Infantry. Following the inspection, the royal limousine proceeded towards the City Hall to the accompaniment of thunderous cheers and the clattering of the brilliant escort of the Royal Canadian Dragoons. In front of the City Hall Their Majesties alighted and walked onto the reception dais. A massed choir of seven hundred voices rendered the National Anthem and 'O Canada'.

The singing over, the Mayor begged His Majesty to accept an illuminated address expressing Hamilton's loyalty, and the Sovereigns inscribed their names on the city visitors' register. Mrs. Morrison presented the Queen with a bouquet of orchids, and Mayor Morrison introduced to Their Majesties the members of the City Council and their wives.

Then Their Majesties walked over to the veterans' stand amidst cheers from the crowd. All along the front rank the Sovereigns strolled, pausing to say a few words to every one of the men in the wheel-chairs. To a naval veteran the Queen said: 'I want you to give the greetings and good wishes of the King and myself to all the veterans of Hamilton.'

King George and Queen Elizabeth then began their drive through streets crowded with enthusiastic bystanders. At the Civic Stadium thirty thousand school children in the stands set up a joyous ovation, while the King and Queen, saluting and smiling, drove along the circling track lined by Boy Scouts, Girl Guides, Cubs, and Brownies. When the Sovereigns approached the dais, the Navy League Cadets presented arms. Then six hundred boys and six hundred girls staged a demonstration of physical culture, exhibiting rhythmic movement and perfect unison, which drew from the King the remark to the Queen: 'This is wonderful.'

Presently Their Majesties re-entered their car, and the band struck up 'Will Ye No Come Back Again', which was sung by the massed choir. Heading towards the Jockey Club Station, the royal procession drove through another mile of thronged streets, decorated buildings, and cheering bystanders. Mayor and Mrs. Morrison, Premier and Mrs. Hepburn took their leave, and the King and Queen waved from the slowly moving train in a last acknowledgement of Hamilton's cheers.

Leaving Hamilton shortly after three o'clock, the blue train had to pick up speed, and could not slow down at Stoney Creek, nor at Winona or Grimsby, despite the cheering crowds, but at Beamsville the Queen waved to the assemblage at the station. Steaming through Vineland and Jordan, which were crowded with onlookers, the train reached St. Catharines at four o'clock.

With twenty thousand people packing the reception grounds, Their Majesties walked down to the red-carpeted platform, hailed with storms of cheers, while the guard of honour from the St. Catharines Collegiate and

Ridley College came to the salute. Mayor Charles Daley and Mrs. Daley greeted Their Majesties, after being presented by the Prime Minister, and welcomed them to St. Catharines. The Royal Standard was broken out by Ben Messler, an eighty-four-year-old veteran. The band of the Lincoln and Welland Regiment played the National Anthem, which the crowd sang.

To His Majesty the Mayor presented an illuminated address of welcome, and his daughter, Miss Maxine Daley, offered to Her Majesty a bouquet of mauve orchids. The city aldermen, the heads of civic departments and public institutions, and the presidents of war veterans' associations and their wives, as well as several natives of Glamis, home of Queen Elizabeth, were intro- duced. The Sovereigns signed the city visitors' book and the guest register of the Niagara-on-the-Lake Historical Society.

In the midst of great farewell cheers, Their Majesties entered their auto- mobile and drove off to Niagara Falls. Along Niagara Street, the royal car slowed down at the place where two blue and silver pylons marked the new highway between St. Catharines and Niagara Falls. Amid tumultuous acclaim it was dedicated by Her Majesty as the royal car broke an electric beam which dropped the draping Union Jacks and revealed the inscription: 'The Queen Elizabeth Way'.

Turning north for the thirty-one-mile scenic drive to Niagara Falls, the royal party first reached Port Weller, where Their Majesties were tumultu- ously welcomed by a large crowd assembled in the vicinity of the first lock of the Welland Ship Canal. The car slowed down, allowing the royal visitors a fine view of the great engineering work.

Lining its streets gay with flags and banners, Niagara-on-the-Lake awaited the royal procession, being joined by thousands of Americans from across the river. Driving through the beautiful green swards and fine trees of the river- side, the royal party paused at Queenston Heights to take a look at Brock's Monument. Circling the driveway, Their Majesties halted for a few minutes, without alighting, at the little gate leading to the monument where there is a good view of the historic stone column. Here history repeated itself, with a slight difference. Again the heights of Queenston were stormed, as in 1812, by Americans. But today they had come to hail a British king. There were thousands of them, including five hundred school children and a cadet corps from Lewiston, New York. They carried small Union Jacks and American flags. The American spectators cheered a hearty welcome to Their Majesties. But the Canadian adults and school children massed at the entrance to the park were not to be outdone. There rose from them a tumult of acclamations which continued as long as King George and Queen Elizabeth remained in view.

On the drive to the city the Sovereigns made only one stop. Getting out of their car, they walked briskly to the cable-car terminus and for a few minutes looked down the awesome gorge to the swirling, foaming waters far below. A short time later, on entering the Victoria Park grounds through the Mowat Gate, the royal car for the second time broke an electric beam, this time unveiling the Canadian corner-stone of the new international bridge being built over the Niagara River. Half a mile farther on, the Sovereigns reached the boundary of Niagara Falls, about quarter to six.

At the boundary the royal party was met by a mounted escort of the Royal Canadian Dragoons, while an artillery salute of twenty-one guns was fired by the St. Catharines Field Battery, R.C.A. All the way through the streets the route, lined with soldiers and American Legionnaires, was packed with shouting spectators. The royal automobile pulled up before the Administration Building of the Niagara Parks Commission, where stood a guard of honour of the Royal Canadian Air Force. Their Majesties were met at the door of the car by Mayor Carl Hanniwell and Mrs. Hanniwell, who were introduced by the Prime Minister, who also presented the Honourable T. B. McQuesten, Ontario Minister of Highways, and C. Ellison Kunneyer, General Manager of the Niagara Parks. The royal visitors were then conducted to the dais on the upper terrace of the building, overlooking a scene of great beauty: white and mauve lilacs flowered in profusion at the entrance to the building, and in the distance, framed in foliage, appeared the tumbling waters of the American Falls, with Goat Island in the background.

To His Majesty Mayor Hanniwell presented an address of welcome from the citizens of Niagara Falls. Her Majesty accepted a bouquet of orchids from six-year-old Eleanor Donald and four-year-old David Hanniwell. The Mayor introduced the members of the City Council and a number of prominent citizens and their wives, and the Honourable T. B. McQuesten presented the members of the Niagara Parks Commission and their wives. The King and Queen then entered the building, where tea was served to the royal party.

After tea, Their Majesties drove to Table Rock for a close-up view of the Falls. The King had seen them once before, twenty-six years earlier, when as 'Corporal Johnson' he visited Niagara with a party of British midshipmen. It was the Queen's first view of the stupendous, awe-inspiring Falls. For ten minutes the royal tourists watched the amazing rush of the water crashing headlong over the brink of the precipice to fall one hundred and sixty-five feet, and the cloud of fine vapour rising from the vortex of the foaming water at the bottom. 'It is absolutely wonderful,' remarked the Queen.

Their Majesties next drove, to the accompaniment of rolling cheers, to the General Brock Hotel, where they proceeded to the balcony on the third floor. As the Sovereigns stepped to the stone balustrade, haloed fortuituously, as it were, by the setting sun, a tornado of acclaiming shouts went up from the twelve thousand school children.

The King and Queen were then escorted to the suite set aside for their use. It was the first opportunity of the day for a period of rest after nine receptions between ten and seven o'clock.

At eight o'clock, the Sovereigns came down to dinner, which, at the King's own request, after the many functions of the day, was an informal affair. Their Majesties occupied chairs on opposite sides of the table, the Queen sitting between Sir Ronald Lindsay, British Ambassador to the United States, and Mr. Daniel C. Roper, United States Minister to Canada. Beside the King were Mrs. Roper and Prime Minister King. Dinner was served in the Rainbow Room, located on the top floor and overlooking both the American and Canadian Falls. As darkness fell over the scene, the beams of great searchlights threw successively different coloured lights over the two falls, creating an eerie atmosphere of fantasy and wonder.

At a certain moment a massed shrill cry: 'We want the King! We want the Queen!' became a steady chanting. At the well-known refrain the King and Queen exchanged a smile, which meant: 'It's the children.' The children it was, twelve hundred of them, from the city of Welland, who had reached Niagara Falls too late to see the King and Queen on the balcony. The chant lasted for some twenty minutes. Then in the Rainbow Room the King said 'I would just love to do it.' And about nine o'clock the King and Queen stepped onto the flood-lit balcony, waving to the children, and the youth of Welland answered with long cheers.

A few minutes later, at 9:10, the Sovereigns drove through streets packed with shouting onlookers to the station, where the King reviewed a double guard of honour of the Lincoln and Welland Royal Canadian Air Force. Their Majesties then walked to the royal train, when Mayor Hanniwell mentioned to the King that in the station waited a ten-coach train carrying twelve hundred school children from Lambton and Middlesex, who, leaving Sarnia at five o'clock that morning, had travelled sixty miles to London, arriving there just in time to see the royal train pulling out. Thanks to the efforts of Mr. Ross Gray, Member of Parliament for Lambton West, it had been arranged by the Canadian National Railways that their train should continue on to Niagara—another one hundred and thirty miles—on the trail of the royal train. So, concluded the Mayor, would Their Majesties be on the rear platform when passing alongside the Sarnia train? At once the King replied: 'We would be awfully glad to do it.'

Boarding their coach, the Sovereigns remained on the observation platform while the royal coach slowly rode along past the Sarnia train, the King and Queen smiling and waving at the Sarnia children who crowded every car step and window, yelling their exultant cheer.

NIAGARA FALLS–WASHINGTON

AT 9:32 IN THE EVENING, June 7, 1939, for the first time in history, a reigning British King entered the United States of America. When the royal train crossed the international boundary on the bridge, a royal salute of guns began booming in the distance. Crowds, gathered at the United States end of the Suspension Bridge—the first Americans to greet Their Majesties on American soil—cheered as the royal coach rolled by. When the locomotive steamed into the station of Niagara Falls, New York, a shout went up from the five hundred spectators packed into the small station ground. From the train Their Majesties stepped down to a red carpet, and the British Ambassador to the United States, Sir Ronald Lindsay, presented to King George and Queen Elizabeth the Secretary of State, the Honourable Cordell Hull, and Mrs. Hull. After shaking hands, Mr. Hull said:

> Your Majesties, on behalf of the Government and the people of the United States, I have the honour and pleasure of extending to you our warmest welcome. All are delighted with your visit. The people of my country, in the most genuine spirit of cordiality, hospitality, and friendliness, have every desire to make your stay a thoroughly enjoyable one.

To the Queen, Mrs. Hull presented a corsage of orchids and said: 'Your Majesty, it is a great honour for me to meet and to greet you.'

After the train had pulled out of Niagara Falls, New York, Queen

Elizabeth came to the door of the royal coach as crossing after crossing was thronged with cheering people to whom the Queen smilingly waved her hand. At Buffalo the King and Queen made a surprise appearance on the rear platform as the train slowly moved through the city, being greeted by small groups along the tracks. A group of persons coming out of a car-loading warehouse spoke to the Sovereigns as they stood on the observation platform. Queen Elizabeth inquired about the place and ended by asking what kind of weather they would encounter in Washington. 'Pretty hot,' one of the men answered. The explicit reply greatly amused the royal couple. 'Thanks all the same,' the King said with a smile.

During the evening journey to Washington a ceremony took place on board the royal train. In his coach the King invested Sir Ronald Lindsay with the Grand Cross of the Order of the Bath. He also conferred the accolade of knighthood, with the insignia of Knight Commander of the Royal Victorian Order, upon Mr. Alan Lascelles, his acting private secretary, and bestowed the insignia of the Commander of the Royal Victorian Order upon Mr. George F. Steward, chief press liaison officer.

The great historic moment of the American tour—the meeting of the King of Great Britain and the President of the United States—came on the arrival of the royal train at Washington's Union Station. King George stepped down from the royal coach to a blue carpet laid from the train to the reception room, and at once a corps of drums and bugles sounded four ruffles and flourishes. As Their Majesties walked down the platform, escorted by Secretary of State Cordell Hull and Sir Ronald Lindsay, cheers rose from the spectators. The Secretary of State made the formal introduction: 'Mr. President, I have the honour to present Their Britannic Majesties.' With a broad smile, President Roosevelt clasped the King's hand and cordially welcomed him: 'Well, at long last, I greet you. How are you? I am glad to see you.'

'Mr. President, it is indeed a pleasure to Her Majesty and myself to be here,' replied the King.

The members of Their Majesties' suite were presented to the President and Mrs. Roosevelt, and the members of the reception committee were presented to the King and Queen. After these presentations, the President with the King, followed by the Queen with Mrs. Roosevelt, led the way out of the reception room to the plaza in front of the station. As the party emerged, a tremendous roar of cheers from the forty thousand people crowding the grounds saluted the royal visitors. Immediately the Marine Band struck up 'God Save the King', followed by 'The Star-Spangled Banner'. As the music ended, the French 75's of the 16th Field Artillery on the outer rim of the plaza began booming a twenty-one-gun salute. Presently the King and the President, conversing and laughing, entered the waiting automobile, the Queen and Mrs. Roosevelt entered a second car, and the royal procession moved off on its way to the White House.

For Their Majesties it was a triumphant drive, to the acclamation of hundreds of thousands of heartily welcoming onlookers. Along the two-and-a-half-mile route three quarters of a million people—almost double the population of Washington—were packed along the curbs. Bright coloured shields bearing the royal coat of arms and the arms of the United States hung from lamp-posts beneath British and American colours. The whole route was lined by six thousand marines, sailors, and soldiers, standing at the salute, and seven bands were stationed at favourable points.

From the station plaza, the procession moved along Delaware Avenue to the Capitol in the midst of tremendous clapping and cheering. The King frequently saluted in acknowledgement, and the President raised his silk hat. On approaching the Capitol, the royal party was acclaimed by the multitude thronging the grounds and Pennsylvania Avenue, which was crowded to capacity, while from the high buildings along the avenue showers of paper streamers and confetti floated down as a greeting to the royal visitors. (These came down in such abundance that one hundred and two men with eighteen trucks were required to clean the streets, and the weight of the paper collected amounted to more than two hundred tons!)

On reaching the White House, the procession drove to the south entrance. A guard of honour formed by four hundred men of the President's Own Regiment—the First Battalion of the Twelfth Infantry—presented arms. The King and the President alighted and waited for the Queen and Mrs. Roosevelt. After presentation of the members of the staff, the royal party entered the White House and proceeded to the East Room, where the members of the Diplomatic Corps had assembled, to be presented to Their Majesties.

After this formal ceremony, which was over by 12:15, Their Majesties were escorted to their private rooms, where they rested for a short time. Then the royal guests came down to the state dining-room for a private luncheon, restricted to guests staying at the White House.

Luncheon over, King George and Queen Elizabeth enjoyed a thirty-one-mile sightseeing tour of Washington. Preceded by a motor-cycle escort and cheered by people along the route, the King often waved to the crowds, while the Queen lifted her hand in greeting, with a smile. The royal party first drove past the Lincoln Memorial. They next paid a brief visit to the Cathedral

Church of St. Peter and St. Paul, and then drove by the Tidal Basin and the cherry trees.

After a brief period of rest at the White House, the King and Queen set out again at five o'clock for the garden party at the British Embassy. In the south grounds of the White House, five thousand Boy Scouts and three thousand Girl Guides greeted King George and Queen Elizabeth with uproarious cheers.

At the British Embassy the King and Queen were greeted by Sir Ronald and Lady Lindsay, and entering the mansion, were escorted to the portico leading to the garden. On the lawns strolled or stood, chatting and waiting, some fourteen hundred guests, Secretaries of State, Senators, Congressmen, State Governors, diplomats, business leaders, and social figures, and their wives. The social event of the royal visit to the United States, the garden party gathered the élite of politics and society.

As Their Majesties stepped into view, the band from H.M.S. *Exeter* (on a visit to Baltimore) struck up 'God Save the King', after which thirty special guests standing on the portico were presented. Then the King and Queen, descending into the garden, mingled with the people. Guided by Sir Ronald and accompanied by some of his suite, the King started on a stroll that took him to the east side of the grounds, while the Queen, escorted by Lady Lindsay and the ladies-in-waiting, walked towards the west. Along the separate paths the King and Queen made their way through the groups, chatting with the guests presented by Sir Ronald or Lady Lindsay.

When tea was over, Their Majesties took their departure. Once again they stepped to the front of the portico. With a smile the Queen graciously waved to the guests and the King bowed. The *Exeter* band played 'God Save the King', and as the music ended, Their Majesties retired, while the distinguished assemblage applauded.

The crowning function of the royal visit was the state dinner given in honour of Their Majesties at which the Sovereign of the British Empire and the President of the United States pledged friendship and expressed hopes for peace in the world.

Their Majesties stood with their hosts at the centre door, where the guests were presented before moving to their places in the dining-room. The presentations over, the President escorted the Queen into the dining-room, and the King accompanied Mrs. Roosevelt.

Before the dessert, the President proposed a toast to His Majesty as follows:

Your Majesties:

In the life of a nation, as in that of an individual, there are occasions that stand out in high relief. Such an occasion is the present one, when the entire United States is welcoming on its soil the King and Queen of Great Britain, of our neighbour Canada, and of all the far-flung British Commonwealth of Nations. It is an occasion for festivities, but it is also fitting that we give thanks for the bonds of friendship that link our two peoples.

I am persuaded that the greatest single contribution our two countries have been enabled to make to civilization, and to the welfare of peoples throughout the world, is the example we have jointly set by our manner of conducting relations between our two nations.

It is because each nation is lacking in fear of the other that we have unfortified borders between us. It is because neither of us fears aggression on the part of the other that we have entered no race of armaments, the one against the other.

The King and I are aware of a recent episode. Two small uninhabited islands in the centre of the Pacific became of sudden interest to the British Empire and to the United States as stepping-stones for commercial airplanes between America and Australasia. Both nations claimed sovereignty. Both nations had good cases. To have entered into a long-drawn-out argument could have meant ill-will between us and delay in the use of the islands by either nation. It was suggested that the problem be solved by the joint use of both islands by both nations, and, by a gentleman's agreement, to defer the question of ultimate sovereignty until the year 1989. The passage of fifty years will solve many problems.

If this illustration of the use of methods of peace, divorced from aggression, could only be universally followed, relations between all countries would rest upon a sure foundation, and men and women everywhere could once more look upon a happy, a prosperous, and a peaceful world.

May this kind of understanding between our countries grow ever closer, and may our friendship prosper. Ladies and gentlemen, we drink to the health of His Majesty, King George VI.

The toast being drunk, the King rose and proposed a toast to the President with the following words:

The visit which The Queen and I are paying you today is something which has been in our minds for many weeks, and, if we have had our moments of anxiety, they have served to make us realize how intensely we have been looking forward to the present occasion. I wish, therefore, in the first place to thank you for your kind invitation and for your still kinder welcome. We have been deeply touched by the manner in which Washington has already received us; and we expect to enjoy every minute of our remaining time in the United States.

From Canada, which we have just left and whither we shall soon return, I bring you today the warm greetings of a neighbour and a trusted friend. From my other Dominions, from the United Kingdom, and from all my Empire, I carry to you expressions of the utmost cordiality and good-will. As I drink a toast to you, Mr. President, I wish you every possible health and happiness. I trust and believe that in years to come, the history of the United States will continue to be marked by that ordered progress and by that prosperity which have been theirs in the past. And I pray that our great nations may ever in the future walk together along the path of friendship in a world of peace.

On the conclusion of the King's words, the guests rose and the toast was duly honoured.

After the dessert, the ladies moved to the Green Room for coffee. A little later the ladies and gentlemen rejoined and moved to the East Room for a musical concert, when some two hundred guests were presented to Their Majesties. The concert had been arranged by Mrs. Roosevelt to illustrate present-day American music, which springs from the three sources of folk, popular, and art music. Afterwards the artists and entertainers were presented to the President and Mrs. Roosevelt and to the King and Queen. And after the guests had gone, the King and the President sat together exchanging views on the international situation.

Next day, at his press conference, President Roosevelt said that his con-versation with the King was 'full and unrestricted, just as it might be between any two private individuals'. As to Their Majesties, the President added: 'They are very, very delightful people.' For her part, Mrs. Roosevelt wrote in her daily article, 'My Day': 'These sovereigns are young, and though the weight of responsibility matures people early, still one does not always find in sovereigns such ability or even desire to comprehend the problems which confront so many people in every country today, and which must be solved before we can feel that the average man and woman can have security and liberty.'

WASHINGTON

SECOND DAY

THE ROYAL GUESTS' second day in Washington opened with an unforeseen engagement. On the suggestion of Mrs. Roosevelt, the Queen agreed to appear at the morning meeting of the women journalists at the White House. The news brought eighty-four newspaperwomen to the Green Room, where Mrs. Roosevelt answered a few questions about the royal visitors. She also mentioned that Her Majesty felt that she could not take part in a press conference, since she had never done so in her own country. Replying to questions, the First Lady added: 'It is unusual to find in one so young so compassionate an understanding of the conditions under which many people live and work.'

After explaining that both the King and Queen were especially concerned about social work, Mrs. Roosevelt, speaking of the royal visit, said: 'It seems to me that it has very great value. In the first place it gives people an opportunity actually to see the rulers of another country and to find out what their interests are and what they believe in. I think the mere furtherance of the desire for peace and better understanding is a very fine thing in a troubled world, and the bringing out of a possibility that nations can find solutions for their differences as they arise is tremendously valuable.'

It was a welcome surprise to the journalists when the King joined the party. Mrs. Roosevelt said: 'Your Majesties, the ladies of the press', and the King and Queen went slowly through the double line of women, saying 'Good morning' and bowing slightly to right and left. As they reached the lobby Mrs. Roosevelt took leave of her guests, who made their way at ten o'clock to the British Embassy for the first official function of the day, a reception of Washington's war veterans and the British colony.

Escorted by police on motor-cycles along streets lined with crowds cheering their passage, Their Majesties drove to the British Embassy, where they were received by Sir Ronald and Lady Lindsay, and the Royal Standard was broken out over the Embassy. As the Sovereigns stepped into the high-columned portico leading to the garden where the ex-servicemen and British citizens were stationed, the veterans shouted 'Long live the King!' and the band of H.M.S. *Exeter* played 'God Save the King'.

Accompanied by the British Ambassador, the King went down the line of veterans, shaking hands and talking with them. The group included several Americans who had fought under the British flag. Indeed, the first to be presented was Dr. Bellenden Seymour Hutcheson, who won the Victoria Cross while serving with the 75th Canadian battalion in the Great War.

The royal party now drove to the Capitol for the reception tendered by the Congress of the United States. All along the route, spectators greeted the Sovereigns with continuous applause. In front of the legislative building more than ten thousand persons crowded the plaza, while around the Capitol steps four thousand invited guests, including the families of senators and congress-men, occupied reserved seats. At eleven o'clock, when Their Majesties, accompanied by the Prime Minister of Canada and the British Ambassador, alighted from their car, the vast assemblage broke into applause and the guard of honour of Marine Corps officers presented arms. A reception committee received the royal guests. Senator Key Pittman, Chairman of the Senate Foreign Relations Committee, greeted the Sovereigns. Inside the rotunda, Senator Pittman introduced to Their Majesties Vice-President John V. Garner and Speaker William Bankhead, and then the members of the Senate in order of seniority, the seventy-four senators present shaking hands with the King and the Queen. Next Representative Sol Bloom took his stand beside the King and presented three hundred and fifty-three members of the House of Rep-resentatives, the presentations slowing down as a result of brief greetings by the representatives or questions by Their Majesties.

After the last congressman had been presented, Their Majesties with a bow and a smile turned to leave the rotunda, while the assemblage burst into hearty cheers lasting until the Sovereigns had passed out of the room. The King, turning to Senator Pittman, said: 'Her Majesty and I are unable to express our appreciation of the universal courtesy and friendship we have received.'

Descending the steps, the King and Queen walked through crowded ranks of eager spectators who cheered as the Sovereigns bowed and smiled to right and left, before taking leave of their hosts and re-entering their car.

From the Capitol, the King and Queen proceeded through streets solidly packed with bystanders towards the Navy Yard to be received by the President on board the presidential yacht U.S.S. *Potomac*. A few minutes past noon, into the square facing the presidential yacht rolled the royal car amidst a cheering crowd jamming every inch of available space, and the royal salute of twenty-one guns thundered in the air. Rear-Admiral George Pettengill, Commander of the Navy Yard, and Lieutenant R. W. Jones, Commander of the *Potomac*, welcomed Their Majesties. The Sovereigns were then piped aboard the yacht, and were greeted at the gangway by the President and Mrs. Roosevelt. The President said to King George: 'Good morning, how are you?' and then, referring to the visit to the Capitol, 'Did it turn out all right?' —'Yes, indeed,' replied the King with a broad smile.

The fifteen-mile trip down the river was very pleasant. The King and Queen lunched with the President and Mrs. Roosevelt. The meal was barely over when Mount Vernon was sighted.

Landing from the presidential yacht at 1:22, Their Majesties with the President and Mrs. Roosevelt passed through a double line of sailors to the waiting automobiles, and drove the several hundred yards from the river to the green slope within Washington's estate where stands the small red brick house surrounded by pine and cedar trees that contains the tomb of Washington.

The whole party gathered outside the tomb, which was opened for Their Majesties. While the Queen, the President, and Mrs. Roosevelt remained outside the iron gates, the King, bare-headed, walked in silence and laid upon the slab in the enclosure a wreath of white lilies, red carnations, and blue iris, to which was attached a card bearing the inscription: 'George, R.I., and Elizabeth, R.' He laid the wreath, took two steps backward, stood with bowed head for a brief moment, and then came out.

Their Majesties then walked up the hill to the white Georgian mansion with its eight-columned porch and open green shutters that was Washington's house. With a garden containing fine trees planted by Washington, Jefferson, and Franklin, it stands on a bluff above the Potomac and commands a splendid view.

Leaving Mount Vernon at 2:15, Their Majesties re-entered their cars with the President and Mrs. Roosevelt for a drive to Fort Hunt Civilian Conservation Corps Camp for Unemployed Youths. On reaching the camp Their Majesties were received by Captain Blair E. Henderson, Camp Commander, and Robert Fechner, Civilian Conservation Corps Director. The King showed at once a keen interest in the organization as a result of his personal knowledge of youth camps in England. He began to ask questions and accepted an invitation to visit the barracks and mess hall. In the course of the inspection, the King inquired about the cuisine, camp training, and enrolment of the boys.

He also examined a display of photographs showing the activities. The King and Queen concluded the visit, which lasted nearly half an hour, by shaking hands and talking with a few of the boys forming a guard of honour.

Shortly after three o'clock, Their Majesties re-entered their cars with the President and Mrs. Roosevelt and motored to the National Cemetery at Arlington to lay a wreath on the Tomb of the Unknown Soldier and on the Canadian Cross.

The Tomb of the Unknown Soldier is at the foot of broad steps leading to the stately Grecian Amphitheatre which forms the Memorial to the symbolic warrior. It occupies a site on tree-studded green slopes overlooking Washington. Full military ritual marked the ceremony. As the two cars carrying the King and the President, the Queen and the First Lady entered the National Cemetery at 3:15, a royal salute of twenty-one guns boomed from the near-by slopes. A few minutes later, Cabinet members and their wives, and British and Canadian members of the royal suite took positions on the steps facing the tomb. Thousands of people crowded the steps and slopes about the Memorial and others filled the amphitheatre at the rear.

Presently the two cars bearing Their Majesties, the President, and Mrs. Roosevelt halted in front of the tomb plaza. While the President stood at the side of his automobile, the King was met by General Malin Craig, Army Chief of Staff, and the Queen and Mrs. Roosevelt by Brigadier-General Maxwell Murray. The Army band played 'God Save the King' and 'The Star-Spangled Banner', and the guard of honour of four squads of soldiers, marines, and sailors presented arms. When the last note had died away, the King was escorted by General Craig to a position in front of the Tomb, which bears the inscription: 'Here rests in honored glory an American soldier known but to God'. From a sergeant in the uniform of the Royal Highlanders of Canada the King received a wreath of white lilies and white carnations, bearing a white card with the names: 'George, R.I., and Elizabeth, R.' The King laid the wreath on the tomb, took four paces backward, and then bowed his head, while the guard of honour presented arms. Then the drums sounded four ruffles, and the ceremony concluded with the sounding of taps by a marine bugler.

From the Tomb of the Unknown Soldier Their Majesties, accompanied by the royal party, ascended the steps into the trophy room and entered the amphitheatre to the cheers of five thousand people seated there. Leaving the building, they descended the green slopes leading to the near-by Canadian Cross, a monolith of Canadian granite twenty-seven feet high, bearing the inscription: 'Canadian Monument erected by the Government of Canada in honor of the United States soldiers who served in the Canadian Army and gave their lives in the Great War, 1914-1918'.

The King and the royal party having reached the Canadian Cross, the Navy band played 'God Save the King' and then 'The Star-Spangled Banner', and the guard of honour presented arms. Then the King moved forward to the Cross and was presented by a member of the staff of the Canadian Legation with a wreath of calla lilies inscribed with the words: 'George, R.I., and Elizabeth, R.' The King walked to the cross and deposited the wreath. Taking three steps backward, he stood with bowed head while a marine drummer rolled taps and a trumpeter sounded the Last Post. During the ceremony, the King was attended by General Craig and the Queen by General Murray, while Prime Minister King accompanied Mrs. Roosevelt.

The ceremony over, the royal party returned to their cars, and the royal automobile, leading the way, was saluted by the booming of twenty-one guns as it left the cemetery. The royal procession motored back to Washington through the Memorial Gate and by way of the Memorial Bridge, reaching the White House about four o'clock.

After a half-hour rest Their Majesties came down to the White House garden for an informal tea with a purpose. The tea had been arranged by Mrs. Roosevelt with a view to informing the King and Queen on the activities of the Roosevelt administration—the New Deal, for short—in its endeavours to solve social and economic problems. The information was to be offered through personal conversations with Cabinet members and heads of Government agencies connected with such policies. Before tea-time was over, every one of the thirty-four guests present had shared in the privilege of a chat with the King or the Queen. They all agreed that the royal couple were well informed about social and economic activities and were keenly interested in means to solve unsatisfactory conditions.

After tea came the first opportunity for relaxation. About six o'clock the King, the President, and Mrs. Roosevelt, accompanied by Elliott and Ruth Roosevelt, stole away and enjoyed a brief respite from the flaming heat of the day by swimming in the pool in the White House grounds.

The last function of one of the busiest days of the royal tour took place in the evening when Their Majesties entertained the President and the First Lady at a state dinner at the British Embassy.

Shortly after eight o'clock the King and Queen departed from the White House, which had been their residence for almost two days. On leaving the presidential mansion, the Queen cast a lingering look around and remarked: 'I wish I could stay longer. I have had a wonderful time.' The royal car drove along streets crowded with spectators eager to have a last look at the royal couple. At the door of the Embassy Their Majesties were greeted by Ambassador and Lady Lindsay, who escorted them to the drawing-room, where the company had already assembled.

Having left the White House ten minutes after Their Majesties, the President and the First Lady arrived at the British Embassy at 8:15. They were received by their hosts, King George and Queen Elizabeth, who walked with them to the drawing-room, where the President and Mrs. Roosevelt were greeted by the other guests.

Shortly after 10:45, Their Majesties temporarily bade good-bye to the President and the First Lady, who left the Embassy and returned to the White House. About 11:15, the Sovereigns drove to the railway station through streets lined all the way with large crowds who shouted a last farewell to the royal visitors. The Secretary of State and Mrs. Hull escorted Their Majesties to the train. There was a last exchange of greetings, a last handshake. The King and Queen mounted the steps of the coach, and the train slowly pulled out on its way to New York to the cheers of the crowd and its friendly cries: 'Come back again!' So ended Their Majesties' visit to Washington, which was aptly epitomized by the *New York Times* in a huge headline: 'The British Take Washington Again'.

NEW YORK CITY

THROUGHOUT THE NIGHT the blue flyer raced northward. From early dawn, groups had assembled at stations to see the royal coach. At nine o'clock it slowly moved into Red Bank, gaily decked with Stars and Stripes and Union Jacks.

Presently the King and Queen descended to the station platform. The welcoming party moved forward, and the British Ambassador presented to Their Majesties Governor A. Harry Moore, of the State of New Jersey, and Mrs. Moore. The Governor said: 'Your Majesties have honoured New Jersey, whose first Governor came from the Isle of Jersey in 1664.' He then presented the King with a copy of a resolution of welcome adopted by the State Legislature on the preceding Monday, June 5. Mrs. Moore offered the Queen a bouquet of orchids, and her niece, five-year-old Jane Margaret Clee, a bouquet of lilies of the valley.

The Mayor of Red Bank and Mrs. English were then presented to Their Majesties. The Mayor welcomed the King, and Mrs. English presented the Queen with a bouquet of delphinia.

As an army band played 'God Save the King', the King saluted and the guard of honour from the 52nd Coast Artillery presented arms. Then the King reviewed the guard of honour and Their Majesties walked to a closed automobile amidst cheers from the crowd. The procession headed for Fort Hancock on Sandy Hook to board the U.S. destroyer *Warrington* in order to approach New York by water, and view the famous Manhattan skyline.

As Their Majesties' car entered the camp at 9:40, a salute of twenty-one guns boomed while ten United States Army planes roared overhead. When the King stepped from his car, Colonel Willieford, Commandant of Fort Hancock, saluted, and the guard of honour from the 16th Infantry presented arms.

Passing through lines of officers and seamen, the Sovereigns walked up the gangplank of the *Warrington*. Their Majesties were welcomed at the rail by Commander Leighton Wood; the Royal Standard was hoisted for the first time in history on an American ship-of-war; and royal salutes were fired from the Shore Battery, from the *Warrington*, and from the cutter *Campbell*.

On emerging from the Narrows into the Upper Bay, the destroyer was greeted by a number of excursion steamers, cabin cruisers, speed boats, and small craft, all gay with bunting. When the *Warrington* passed Governor's Island, a twenty-one-gun salute was fired from Fort Jay. Soon the royal visitors could see New York's fantastic line of towering skyscrapers. As the *Warrington* entered the inner harbour of New York, hundreds of large and small vessels, flying Union Jacks and Stars and Stripes, incessantly blew their whistles and sirens and clanged their bells in a shrieking welcome.

At 11:19, amidst the clamorous noise of ships' whistles, the roar of aeroplanes, music of bands, and shouts of welcome from scores of thousands of spectators, the *Warrington* tied up to Pier I in front of the New York Battery, while a twenty-one-gun salute was fired by the Coast Guard cutter *Campbell*, which had escorted the destroyer. Saluted by the crew lining the side of the ship, the Sovereigns came down the gangway into the landing-shed, which was decorated with British and American flags, and walked along the red carpet stretching from the shipside to the waiting automobile.

As Their Majesties entered the long, open automobile for the drive to the World's Fair, the crowds burst into long, loud cheers, which the Queen acknowledged with a smile, while the King stood and waved his hand. From the nearest skyscrapers fluttered down showers of ticker-tape and paper streamers in typical New York welcome. The procession of fifty automobiles drew slowly away from the Battery and ascended a ramp to the West Side Highway, which was lined with half a million cheering men, women, and children. At the suggestion of the King, the driving speed was reduced to give the people a better opportunity to see the royal couple.

Farther uptown, the King and Queen were able to view the mid-town section with its towering buildings, the tremendous bulk of the Rockefeller Center, the sky-piercing Empire State Building, and the gleaming spire of the Chrysler Building.

At 12:40 King George and Queen Elizabeth passed through the World's Fair gate, and the automobile drove up to Perylon Hall, where Mr. Grover A. Whalen, President of the Fair Corporation, and Mrs. Whalen were presented to Their Majesties and welcomed them to the World's Fair. The King and Queen, with the members of the royal party, proceeded to the reception room, which was laid with a carpet that had once belonged to Louis XIV, and was hung with a Gobelin tapestry. Their Majesties sat on a dais in two chairs made for Louis XVI. After they had signed their names in the Fair's guest book, the King was presented by Mr. Whalen with a solid gold trylon and crystal glass perisphere, with a thermometer in the trylon and a clock in the perisphere. The Queen was presented with a corsage of orchids by Mrs. Harvey D. Gibson.

Then, walking out of Perylon Hall, the King and Queen took their places in a trackless train, with the members of the royal party. Preceded by a mounted guard of honour of Herskell Indians in scarlet uniforms, the royal car toured the Fair Grounds between deep rows of cheering spectators.

The procession halted in the vast Court of Peace. The Sovereigns then walked across the court between a marine and army guard of honour to the Federal Building. At the main entrance Mr. Whalen presented to Their Majesties Mr. Edward J. Flynn, United States Commissioner General to the Fair, and Mrs. Flynn. After the royal party had entered the building and proceeded to the reception room, twenty guests were presented to Their Majesties, and the Sovereigns then moved to the state dining-room for luncheon.

About 2:50, at the close of the luncheon, as Their Majesties came out, heralds in blue and gold sounded their trumpets from the roof-tops of the

Hall of Nations. The King and Queen stood for several minutes on the terrace, being warmly greeted by the multitude thronging the Court of Peace. Then they passed through a guard of honour of thirty Boy Scouts and thirty Girl Guides—the latter being all thirteen years of age in honour of thirteen-year-old Girl Guide Princess Elizabeth—and began their visits of the various pavilions of the British Empire.

The Sovereigns walked the short distance to the Irish Pavilion, where the Irish Commissioner General, Mr. Leo T. MacAuley, was presented; he greeted Their Majesties and in turn presented the members of his staff. The Sovereigns were escorted around the exhibits and signed their names in the book of distinguished visitors.

Emerging from the pavilion, the Sovereigns boarded a flag-decked electric train which carried them to the Canadian Building. In front of that pavilion, in a splash of colour, stood the guard of forty red-coated members of the Royal Canadian Mounted Police. At the entrance they were greeted by the Honourable W. D. Euler, Canadian Minister of Trade and Commerce. The King and Queen were specially interested in an illuminated map of Canada, on which they retraced the route they had followed during their Canadian tour. As they left the building, the Sovereigns paused to speak to a few veterans and war nurses, the place of honour being reserved to an American, Thomson Reeve, of Buffalo, who holds the Victoria Cross. Then Their Majesties walked into the adjacent building, containing an exhibition of Canadian art.

Re-boarding the electric cars, the royal party proceeded to the Australian Pavilion. The Commissioner General, Mr. L. R. MacGregor, and Mrs. Mac-Gregor were presented to Their Majesties. Passing in front of a small guard of honour of war veterans, the royal visitors entered the building, where one hundred and forty Australians were awaiting their visit. The King and Queen made a tour of the exhibits.

Passing to the adjacent New Zealand Pavilion, Their Majesties were greeted by the Commissioner General, Mr. Roberts, Mr. Firth, and Mrs. Firth, who were presented by the British Ambassador.

Entering the trackless train once more, the royal party rode across the Lagoon of Nations, where dense masses of people sent up roars of cheers. The procession halted at the British Pavilion. Several hundred guests facing the building applauded the royal couple. Presented by British Ambassador Sir Ronald Lindsay, the British Commissioner General, Sir Louis Beale, and Lady Beale escorted Their Majesties to the building. Walking between ranks of a guard of honour of British veterans of the Great War, the King chatted with Captain Harold Austen, a Victoria Cross holder, who told the King that during the Great War he was sinking German submarines. 'How many did you sink?' asked the King.—'Well, Sir, I was paid for sinking two,' came the reply. The King laughed and passed on to another veteran, while the Queen was talking with some war nurses.

As they entered the pavilion, the royal visitors stopped to read the inscription: 'This building is dedicated to the lasting peace and friendship between the peoples of the United States of America and the British Empire.'

Leaving the British Pavilion amidst volleys of cheers, Their Majesties returned to their automobile for the drive to Columbia University, for its official reception. On reaching the University, a few minutes before five o'clock, the royal car stopped in front of the Low Memorial Library, which was surrounded by an immense multitude of spectators, while more than five thousand professors and students waited on the campus. Greeted by cheers, Their Majesties were received at the curb by the President of the University, Dr. Nicholas Murray Butler, in academic robes, who presented Mr. Frederick Coykendall, Chairman of the Trustees. Ascending the library steps, the King and Queen went into the building and were escorted by Dr. Butler to the dais, as the string orchestra played Elgar's 'Pomp and Circumstance'. There was general applause from the audience of five hundred guests, university trustees, and faculty members. Then Dr. Butler addressed the royal visitors:

'Your Majesties, I have the honour to present the members of the University Council, its trustees, representatives of every school, members of the Affiliated Corporation and guests of the University, who have assembled to greet you on this occasion.'

The President read an address of welcome on behalf of the University, and the orchestra played 'God Save the King'. After examining the original charter granted to the University as King's College in 1754, the King and Queen signed their names in the distinguished visitors' book. As Their Majesties returned to the dais, the orchestra struck up 'The Star-Spangled Banner'. The music being over, Their Majesties moved out of the room, accompanied by Dr. Butler, amidst applause from the audience. They proceeded to their waiting automobile and, after shaking hands with Dr. Butler, took leave of their hosts of the day, Governor and Mrs. Lehman and Mayor and Mrs. LaGuardia. Entering a closed automobile, the Sovereigns, to the cheers of many thousands of spectators, departed for a drive through the countryside to the President's home at Hyde Park.

The impressions of the royal visit to New York were summed up in the evening by Mayor LaGuardia: 'As I left the royal couple at Columbia University, I told the King that I thought their visit had negotiated a treaty of friendship that would take many years to revoke and that his visit did more good than the sending of a dozen ambassadors or the interchange of fifty diplomatic notes.'

HYDE PARK

FROM POUGHKEEPSIE, the last town on the route, to Hyde Park, Their Majesties drove between rows of cheering spectators. At 7:40 the royal car halted in front of the grey stone Georgian house of the Roosevelt estate.

Rather wearied by the very busy and hot day in New York, the King and Queen doubly enjoyed the cool atmosphere and hearty welcome of the place, when the President and Mrs. Roosevelt, and the President's eighty-four-year-old mother, Mrs. Sarah Roosevelt, came out on the columned porch to greet them. The King started to apologize for being so late, but, broadly smiling, the President replied: 'Kings are never late. Dinner was announced for eight o'clock, but it was not expected to be served before nine. So there is plenty of time ahead.'

Presently the King and Queen were escorted to their rooms on the second floor for a period of rest before dinner. Then, at half past nine, refreshed, they sat down to dinner with the President and Mrs. Roosevelt.

Next morning was Sunday, June 11. It was the last day of the royal tour of the United States and the most informal day of the whole visit to America, for there was no official programme of any kind. Shortly before eleven o'clock Their Majesties left for St. James Episcopal Church, Hyde Park, in which three generations of Roosevelts have worshipped and of which the President was the senior warden.

The service was very simple. A collect and two lessons were read, and four hymns were sung. The sermon was preached by Dr. Henry St. George Tucker, Bishop and Head of the Episcopal Church in the United States. The service concluded with the customary prayer for the President, which was followed by a prayer for Their Majesties, Queen Mary, and the two Princesses.

Back at the Roosevelt home, King George and Queen Elizabeth spoke over the telephone to their daughters in London. Princesses Elizabeth and Margaret Rose were overjoyed, and plied their parents with questions. They were much amused to know that their mother and father were about to go to lunch, when Margaret Rose was about to go to bed.

A picnic luncheon took place at President Roosevelt's own cottage, three miles from his mother's mansion. The picnic party was as cheerful as it was informal, the royal couple looking rested and comfortable. At the cottage, which is of plain field stone, with a large veranda, Their Majesties were greeted by Mrs. Roosevelt. The other guests had already arrived and were waiting about the grounds.

The King and Queen, with the chief guests, took their seats at seven tables on the veranda. The Queen sat at the first table with the President and Mrs. Herbert H. Lehman and Secretary of the Treasury Morgenthau. The King headed the second table, having with him the President's mother, Mrs. Morgenthau, and Governor Lehman. The picnic fare included cold ham, smoked roast turkey, lettuce-and-tomato salad, baked beans, and brown bread, as well as hot and iced coffee and iced tea. Heading the menu were hot dogs.

Following the picnic, an entertainment was given by two Oklahoma Indians. In beaded buckskin costumes, a girl dancer, Te-Ata, and a singer, Ish-Ti-Opi, interpreted some folk tales and songs.

About four o'clock the picnic party dispersed, and Their Majesties and President Roosevelt motored with other members of the royal party to Mrs. Sarah Roosevelt's cottage, Val-Kill, which is only a short distance away from the Roosevelt mansion. The day was very hot, with the temperature hovering around ninety-five degrees, and both the King and the President went for a swim in the spring-fed tile swimming-pool. The Queen and Mrs. Roosevelt with other guests remained about the lawn and were served tea under the trees.

After tea at Val-Kill, the President drove the King and Queen, with his daughter-in-law Mrs. James Roosevelt, to the flat land bordering the Hudson River to view a stand of first-growth timber on his estate, in which the President took great pride. Thence the party drove back to the Roosevelt mansion, arriving there at 6:10.

Before dinner at eight o'clock, the King and Queen descended to the library with neatly wrapped packages. With the dinner guests present, the King stepped up to the President and with a few words handed him a box containing a silver-framed autographed portrait of himself. The Queen presented a similar photo of herself to Mrs. Roosevelt and one to the President's mother. (The President and Mrs. Roosevelt had given photographs of themselves to Their Majesties before the royal visitors left the White House. Mrs. Roosevelt had also given the Queen a set of china.)

The farewell dinner party was given by the President's mother and was restricted to twenty-two persons. It was a pleasant and intimate party. The King and the President exchanged many remarks, repartee sparkled across the table, and there was much laughter amongst the guests. During dinner there was a thunderstorm, and the Queen remarked that this completed the cycle of weather they had experienced during their tour: ice and snow at White River, rain in Winnipeg and Moose Jaw, great heat in Washington, and lightning and thunder with high winds at Hyde Park.

A few minutes before taking leave of Mrs. Sarah Roosevelt, the King presented President Roosevelt with a massive silver inkstand bearing the royal coat of arms. From the Canadian Prime Minister the President received a large silver bowl.

About quarter to eleven Their Majesties left the Roosevelt mansion for the small railway station of Hyde Park, where the blue train was waiting to take them back to Canada for their tour of the Maritime Provinces. The President and Mrs. Roosevelt and the President's mother accompanied their royal guests to the station. In spite of the rain and thunderstorm, more than one thousand people jammed the ground and adjacent street round the station.

The leave-taking was quite informal, much like the breaking-up of a family party. The King and Queen said good-bye and expressed their thanks to the President and the First Lady and to Mrs. Sarah Roosevelt. They took leave also of the British Ambassador and Lady Lindsay. Then the Sovereigns mounted the rear platform of their coach and stood waving to the presidential party and the spectators, while the royal train pulled out.

Dated the next day from Baltimore, which was reached during the night, the following message was sent to the President from King George:

> The Queen and I are deeply grateful, Mr. President, to Mrs. Roosevelt and yourself, for your hospitality during the past four days.
>
> The kindness shown to us personally by you both was endorsed by your fellow countrymen and countrywomen with a cordiality that has stirred our hearts.
>
> In Washington, in New York, and, indeed, wherever we have been in the United States, we have been accorded a reception of which the friendliness was unmistakable.
>
> Though this was our first visit to your great country and though it was

necessarily only a brief one, it has given us memories of kindly feeling
and goodwill that we shall always treasure.

To you, our host, and to the many thousands of American citizens
who also showed us such true hospitality and such spontaneous courtesy,
we send our heartfelt thanks and our best wishes.

                                                              GEORGE, R.I.

Thus came to an end the first visit of a British King and Queen to the
United States, of which the *New York Herald-Tribune* said that it deserved
'to rank as a landmark along this welcome path of English-speaking accord'.
The editorial added: 'Liking so thoroughly this manly and courteous English-
man and his winning Scottish wife, Americans can hardly fail to understand
better and to like better the peoples they so admirably represent.' The *New
York Times* also remarked that the warmth of the welcome that the United
States gave King George and Queen Elizabeth 'does voice an ardent desire
for peace and friendship, for sympathetic understanding and for unity of
two strong nations in a distracted world.'

Across the ocean, the *Yorkshire Post* expressed a similar conclusion: 'This
spontaneous enthusiasm, which sets a seal on an extraordinarily successful
visit, was due in the first place to the combination of ease and dignity with
which the King and Queen made an instant and triumphant appeal to the
heart of the American Republic, but apart from that personal success was
the consciousness that the two English-speaking peoples, albeit they work
under different constitutions, do in fact stand fundamentally for the same
things.'

QUEBEC

AT 5:37 MONDAY MORNING, June 12, the royal train halted briefly at the
border station of Rouse's Point, and then crossed back into Canada.
Steaming by a few stations where groups of farmers stood with their families,
the royal train arrived at St. Jean at 9:25. During the night a violent storm
had played havoc with decorations and signs. But St. Jean had refused to
surrender: debris was cleared away, and new decorations went up. The day

had been declared a civic holiday, and forty thousand people—twice the town's population—jammed the station grounds and the adjoining park.

Their Majesties stepped down to the reception stand, acclaimed with an ovation. The massed bands played 'God Save the King'. No presentations had been expected, as St. Jean did not appear on the official programme, but the King had sent word that he would like to meet the city officials. So Prime Minister King presented to Their Majesties Mayor and Madame Georges Fortin. Then seven-year-old Suzette Lebeau presented a bouquet of orchids to the Queen, who, after asking her her name, kissed her on the cheek and said: 'Tu es délicieuse.'

When the presentations were concluded, Their Majesties walked over to the group of veterans, shaking hands and chatting with them while the crowd kept shouting: 'Vive le Roi! Vive la Reine!'

After a stop of eighteen minutes, the Sovereigns returned to the train and stood on the coach platform, waving to the crowd, while the school children sang 'O Canada', and the train pulled away.

From St. Jean the royal train rushed eastward, being hailed by expectant throngs at small stations. At Sherbrooke, the day had been declared a civic holiday. From all over the district, by tens of thousands, people had converged on the city. Headed by Governor D. Aitken of Vermont, and United States Senator Joseph Montmigny of Lowell, Massachusetts, more than ten thousand New Englanders had invaded Sherbrooke. By eleven o'clock one hundred thousand people were jamming the two-mile route of hilly streets which blazed with decorations and banderoles bearing French and English words of welcome. Fifteen hundred veterans lined the route, with two thousand militiamen.

The royal train rolled into Sherbrooke at 11:50, to the acclaim of the waiting crowds. Governor Aitken of Vermont and Mrs. Aitken occupied seats in a reserved section with the reeves and councillors of neighbouring municipalities. The King and Queen having alighted, Prime Minister King presented Mayor M. T. Armitage and Miss Margaret Armitage, who welcomed the Sovereigns to Sherbrooke. The guns of the 35th Field Battery, R.C.A., boomed a royal salute, and a military band struck up the National Anthem. Miss Armitage presented the Queen with an armful of roses. Then the Chanteclerc singers broke into the Quebec song of 'Alouette'. The Queen listened with a smile and told Miss Armitage standing beside her that 'Alouette' was one of her favourite songs and that she sang it frequently to the little Princesses.

Mayor Armitage presented to Their Majesties the aldermen and their

wives. Then, after signing the city visitors' book, the Sovereigns strolled
along the line of veterans and talked with them, while the crowd kept
cheering. Their Majesties then stepped into the waiting automobile for a
tour of the city. The drive through crowded streets was one continuing wave
of acclamation, especially at points where school children were assembled.

Returning to the station, the royal car was hailed by the thousands of
spectators still in their places. Taking leave of their official hosts, the Sovereigns stood and waved from the platform of their coach amidst a storm of
applause intermingled with cries of 'Vive le Roi! Vive la Reine!'

Every station along the line was jammed with crowds cheering the
passage of the royal train. A warm ovation was extended to the Sovereigns
when the train passed slowly through Thetford Mines at 2:32 p.m. Twenty
thousand people had congregated around the station, and the town was gay
with banners and bunting. When the blue train came into view, Thetford
Mines' acclaim rent the air as long as Their Majesties remained visible.

Farther on, at Charny, the whole population of the village and neigh-
bourhood—several thousand strong—was at the station. At 5:10, the blue
train rolled in, with the the crowd shouting: 'Vive le Roi! Vive la Reine!'
When Their Majesties came out, the children started singing the National
Anthem in French. Then a little five-year-old girl, Noémie Gilbert, was lifted
to the platform railing and presented an armful of flowers to the Queen,
who spoke to her in French. The King chatted briefly with Lieutenant J. L.
Dussault, and asked for Mayor Arcand to be presented. Soon after, amidst
the acclamations of Charny, the Sovereigns departed with farewell waves
to the assemblage.

At St. Romauld the station was thronged with people, and for the last
four miles the tracks were lined with cheering spectators, until the royal
flyer drew into the station at Lévis at 5:41. A multitude crowded all space
around the station, which was hung with flags and bunting, while hundreds
followed the royal coach along the tracks so closely that the police had to
lock arms to hold them back.

When the King and Queen walked to the red-carpeted platform, an
ovation broke loose. A royal salute was fired by the 59th Heavy Battery,
C.F.A., and a military band played the National Anthem. Their Majesties
were greeted by the Lieutenant-Governor of Quebec and Madame Patenaude
and Premier Duplessis.

The royal party proceeded to the reception stand, in front of which
stood a guard of honour formed by the Lévis Regiment, flanked by a contingent of three hundred war veterans. Mayor Durand presented to the King

an illuminated address of welcome and loyalty in both French and English on behalf of the citizens of Lévis. The King and Queen next signed the city visitors' book. Then Mayor Durand presented to Their Majesties the city councillors and their wives, and a number of other citizens.

The presentations over, Their Majesties stepped down from the official stand and moved to the monument prepared to commemorate the royal visit to Lévis. The King unveiled the monument with its bronze plaque bearing the inscription: 'Pour commémorer la visite de Leurs Majestés le roi George VI et la reine Elizabeth à Lévis. Le 12 juin 1939'.

Their Majesties then returned to the train, where they exchanged fare-wells with Lieutenant-Governor and Madame Patenaude, Mayor and Madame Durand, and Premier Duplessis.

Darkness had completely fallen when at 8:32 the blue train glided into Rivière-du-Loup. Thirty thousand people crowded the station square. In front of the dais, as a guard of honour, were lined up a hundred war veterans.

The Prime Minister, amidst long cheers, presented to Their Majesties Mayor and Madame Antonio Paradis, who greeted the Sovereigns and escorted them to the reception stand, while the twelve hundred school children sang the National Anthem. Then Mayor Paradis asked His Majesty to accept an address of welcome, beautifully illuminated and enclosed in a specially-made album containing portraits of Princesses Elizabeth and Margaret Rose, and bearing the coat of arms of Rivière-du-Loup.

Once the presentations were over, the King and Queen walked along the line of the war veterans, to whom they spoke in French, shaking hands with all of them. Then, amidst a continuous storm of applause, the King and Queen re-turned to their observation platform, from which they waved farewell to Rivière-du-Loup, as the train continued on its way to the Maritime Provinces.

NEW BRUNSWICK

TUESDAY, JUNE 13, the royal train invaded New Brunswick. About three o'clock in the morning it made its first stop, at Campbelltown, where, in the gloom, more than three hundred citizens, led by Mayor C. W. Caldwell and the town councillors, congregated at the station. They stood in silence while the locomotive was being serviced; then, when it had pulled out a short distance, they gave three lusty cheers and went back to bed.

When the blue train steamed into the station at Newcastle a great acclaim rose from the spectators. Prime Minister Mackenzie King was first to alight from the train. Presently the King and Queen descended to the platform, and the band of the North Shore Regiment played the National Anthem. The Prime Minister presented to Their Majesties Mayor and Mrs. Creaghan and the Honourable W. S. Anderson, Provincial Minister of Public Works, who represented the Government of New Brunswick, and Mrs. Anderson. Amidst continuous cheers from the crowd, Their Majesties took their places on the red-carpeted reception stand. Mayor Creaghan introduced to them the aldermen and their wives, F. A. Menzies, Warden of Northumberland County, and Miss Menzies.

Then the Mayor presented to the King an address of welcome on behalf of the Town of Newcastle, and Warden Menzies asked His Majesty to accept an address from the County of Northumberland. Then, the official ceremony over, the Sovereigns walked to the veterans, shaking hands and chatting with a number of them, while the spectators cheered them again and again.

Entering their automobile, Their Majesties departed for a two-and-a-half-mile drive through Newcastle. Preceded by a motor-cycle escort of scarlet-coated Mounted Police, the King and Queen rode through streets gaily decorated, spanned by arches of evergreen, and lined by militiamen, Boy Scouts, and Girl Guides, while the bystanders acclaimed their passing with flag-waving and cheers.

It was just past 9:45 when the royal procession left Newcastle for the one-hundred-and-eight-mile drive to Fredericton, through the valley of the Miramichi. Wild shrubs and flowers added a colourful touch to the road-sides, especially the pretty sheep laurel, the mauve blossom of which was greatly admired by Queen Elizabeth, who asked for seeds to be planted in Buckingham Palace gardens.

No official reception was scheduled during the drive. But the village of Millerton tendered such a welcome to Their Majesties that they wished to acknowledge it by an impromptu stop. The decorations stretched over half a mile, with a double row of spruce trees flying small flags, interspersed with several arches of firs adorned with bunting. More than five thousand people hailed Their Majesties with lusty cheers. In front of the Anglican church, where six hundred school children unloosed a barrage of shrill acclamations, the Sovereigns ordered the car to stop, and little Eleanor Flett presented a bouquet of roses to the Queen, amidst the cheers of the crowd and the peals of the church bell.

Shortly after eleven o'clock the royal procession slowed down through Doaktown, where a great arch of green foliage was surrounded by cheering villagers. Just outside the village the King and Queen made an extempore stop at Gilk's House, a small white inn, where tea was served.

Fredericton's broad streets were ablaze with decorations. Never before had the provincial capital been invaded by such throngs of festive people, pouring into the city from all over the province. By noon the streets were solidly packed with spectators, probably fifty thousand in all, quadrupling the city's normal population. Throughout the route of the royal procession were stationed militiamen, war veterans, Boy Scouts, and Girl Guides. It was just past one o'clock when the open car bearing Their Majesties entered the capital of New Brunswick. On sighting the royal procession, the crowds launched into great cheers, while a royal salute of twenty-one guns, fired by the 104th Field Battery, R.C.A., boomed from the grounds of the Canadian Legion.

Moving slowly between deep rows of enthusiastic spectators, the royal procession made its way along Carleton Street and then along Queen Street, until it reached the Parliament Building, in front of which was massed a huge crowd.

As Their Majesties stepped from their automobile in front of the Parliament Building, the band struck up the National Anthem. The Sovereigns were greeted by Prime Minister King, who presented to them Lieutenant-Governor MacLaren and Miss Margaret MacLaren, Premier A. A. Dysart and Mrs. Dysart, and Mayor C. Hedley Forbes and Mrs. Forbes.

Escorted by Lieutenant-Governor MacLaren and Premier Dysart, Their Majesties, moving up the main walk, passed through the portals of the Parliament Building and entered the Assembly Chamber, which was tastefully adorned with large baskets of peonies. After Their Majesties had taken their places in front of the two thrones on the carpeted dais, with the royal suite drawn up on both sides, Premier Dysart presented to the King on behalf of the Province an illuminated address of welcome. His Majesty then handed to Premier Dysart his written reply. Voicing his pleasure in his visit to New Brunswick, the King mentioned his regret at not being able 'to see more of the people, the natural resources and the scenic beauty of this Province'.

Then Mayor Forbes stepped forward and presented to His Majesty an illuminated parchment address of welcome and loyalty on behalf of the citizens of Fredericton. After having received this address, His Majesty handed Mayor Forbes an autographed coloured photograph of Their Majesties as a souvenir of the royal visit to Fredericton.

Then, the King and Queen having stepped down from the dais, Premier Dysart presented to them the Bishop of Fredericton, the Chief Justice of New Brunswick, other judges, the members of his Cabinet, and all their wives.

These and other presentations being over, Premier Dysart asked Their Majesties to sign the Bible that had been donated to Christ Church Cathedral by Edward VII, the King's grandfather, on the occasion of his visit to Fredericton in 1860.

Throughout the ceremony in the Chamber could be heard the continuous chant of the children outside: 'We want the King! We want the Queen!' When the Sovereigns emerged from the Parliament Building, they were thunderously acclaimed by the excited youngsters. Their Majesties stood for a few moments while the children sang the National Anthem. Then, accompanied by the Premier and the Officer in Command, the King moved over to a guard of honour of one hundred Great War veterans and inspected them, stopping to talk with several of the veterans. Standing by the Legion's Colour were two holders of the Victoria Cross: Corporal Herman J. Good, of West Bathurst, and Lieutenant William H. Metcalf, of Eastport, Maine. They were presented to the King.

The inspection over, the King and Queen entered the royal car for the drive to the Lady Beaverbrook Building for the luncheon given by the Provincial Government. They were met at the door of the Lady Beaverbrook Building by the Lieutenant-Governor and Miss MacLaren, and Premier and Mrs. Dysart.

After the luncheon, King George and Queen Elizabeth entered their car for a drive through the city. On reaching the grounds of the Victoria Public Hospital, the Queen caught sight of the patients and nurses assembled on the lawn. She at once spoke to the chauffeur, and the car slowed, continuing at a snail's pace until past the hospital grounds.

Farther on, Their Majesties were accorded a special whooping welcome by one hundred and fifty Micmac and Maliceet Indians, dressed in buckskin, eagle feathers, and ermine skins, gathered in a body on Brunswick Street.

The last part of the drive took the royal visitors along the picturesque river front, to the suburban station of Salamanca, which was surrounded by a crowd of over six thousand people. Here the Lieutenant-Governor, the Premier, and the Mayor took leave of Their Majesties amidst the continuous cheering of the spectators. As the royal train slowly pulled out of the station, the King and Queen stood on the coach platform, waving to the cheering onlookers, while the last guns of the Royal Artillery salute could still be heard in the distance.

From Fredericton to Saint John Their Majesties did not travel on the blue train, as it was considered too heavy for the permanent way of this branch line. Instead, they boarded a smaller train, consisting only of a drawing-room car and four day-coaches. At all stations large groups of cheering people were assembled.

The whole population of Saint John—fifty thousand—, augmented by visitors from all over the province and twelve thousand Americans, seemed to have taken to the streets, so great were the crowds lining the nine-mile route of the procession. Flags flew from decorated buildings, and the route was lined by several thousand guards: militiamen, naval reserves, veterans, city police and firemen, cadets, and Boy Scouts.

The day began at Fairville Station, where the crowd of waiting thousands sent up roars of cheers when the Sovereigns alighted from the train. Prime Minister King presented to Their Majesties Mayor D. L. MacLaren, wearing his gold chain of office, and Mrs. MacLaren.

In a few moments the royal party had assembled on the reception platform, facing which stood a guard of honour formed by the Royal Canadian Naval Reserve and a colour party of war veterans. The Mayor asked the King to accept the city's illuminated address of loyalty, and Mrs. MacLaren presented to Her Majesty a bouquet of pink bouvardia and roses. The brief formalities concluded with the playing of the National Anthem by the band and the firing of a royal salute by the 104th Field Battery, R.C.A., from old Fort Howe.

Then Their Majesties entered the limousine in the midst of applause and started on their visit to Saint John. Entering Saint John proper, the Sovereigns received rousing acclaim from the crowds massed on both sides of the route. When the royal automobile stopped in front of Government House, Their Majesties were cheered by crowds that occupied all available space. They were greeted by Lieutenant-Governor MacLaren, who escorted them along the red carpet lined by a guard of honour of Boy Scout leaders—all holders of the King's badge—drawn from all sections of the province.

Entering flag-draped Government House, Their Majesties walked to the drawing-room, which was banked with baskets of roses and blue violets. Accompanied by Prime Minister Mackenzie King, the Honourable J. E. Michaud, Premier Dysart, and Mrs. Dysart, they sat down to tea, after which the King presented to Premier Dysart autographed royal photographs.

After a fifteen-minute stop, Their Majesties left Government House and returned to their limousine. Noticing the volunteer guard formed by members of the Red Chevron Club and other war veterans, they paused for several minutes to chat with some of the ex-servicemen.

Their Majesties re-entered their car for a drive through the city, and the spectators crowding the sidewalks hailed the Sovereigns all the way to Barrack Green. There Mayor MacLaren and Mrs. MacLaren greeted Their Majesties at the foot of the reception platform. When the King and Queen had ascended the stand, the band struck up the National Anthem and a choir of fifteen hundred children sang it beautifully.

Then Mayor MacLaren presented to Their Majesties forty-one prominent citizens. The presentations over, the King and Queen descended from the platform and, amidst tremendous cheering, walked over to the line of ex-servicemen, all members of the New Brunswick branch of the Canadian Amputation Association of the Great War, headed by Lieutenant-Colonel Beverly R. Armstrong, who presented the veterans. Their Majesties went along the line of veterans, giving each a hearty handclasp and conversing with each for a few moments, and then moved back to speak to the overseas nursing sisters.

Their Majesties having returned to the platform, the children's choir rendered 'O Canada' with great spirit. When the Sovereigns moved to their car, the thousands of spectators joined in an outburst of cheering, as the car slowly drove out of Barrack Green, on its way to the station through streets thronged with cheering spectators.

At the station, after the band had played the National Anthem, the King inspected the guard of honour of the Saint John Fusiliers in white helmets and scarlet tunics. When the official hosts had taken their leave, Their Majesties stood on the observation platform of their coach amidst a storm of cheers, and cries of 'Don't forget to come back and see us.' This was but continuing the words of the banner fronting the station: 'We are very sorry to have you go.'

Hardly out of Saint John, the train made an unscheduled ten-minute stop three miles farther on at Coldbrook, where more than two hundred residents rushed to the rear of the royal coach when, in answer to their acclamation, the King and Queen came to the observation platform, cheered by the delighted spectators.

Skirting Kennebecasis Bay, the train met with a novel reception at Renforth, where three thousand people had gathered. When the royal coach drew up opposite the Renforth Clubhouse, the combined fleets of the Royal Kennebecasis Yacht Club, the Saint John Power Boat Club, and the Rothesay

Yacht Club formed a line of parade. A royal salute of twenty-one guns was fired, and all ensigns were dipped and hoisted again. The Queen stood on the rear platform and King George in the doorway, both waving in salutation.

Through the beautiful countryside the royal train steamed at a good speed, hailed by crowds at every station. At Hampton a large assemblage cheered the train as the King and Queen came out onto the observation platform.

At Sussex, where the train stopped for servicing, ten thousand spectators swarmed round the flag-decorated station, chanting 'We want the King! We want the Queen!' When the Sussex band had finished playing the National Anthem, the royal couple came out and moved down to the platform.

After being presented by Prime Minister King, Mayor William MacLeod and Mrs. McLeod greeted Their Majesties on behalf of the Town of Sussex and the Counties of Kings and Queens. The Mayor presented to the Sovereigns the town councillors and head officials and their wives. Then Beth McQuin presented Her Majesty with a bouquet of lilacs and with a silver teaspoon for each of the Princesses from the Sussex Brownies and Guides.

In response to the popular greetings, Their Majesties started to walk along the platform. Coming to a group of veterans, they exchanged a few words with them. Then the Sovereigns ascended to their coach, remaining on the observation platform waving to the cheering crowd as the train moved out of the station.

During the run between Sussex and Moncton, Their Majesties entertained Prime Minister King at a private dinner, at the close of which the Prime Minister presented some gifts in the name of Canada: a scarf of silver fox for the Queen, two white foxes for Queen Mary, a marten cape and muff for Princess Elizabeth and Princess Margaret Rose. Each gift was packed in a separate cedar box.

It was just shortly after nine o'clock at night when the royal train pulled into Moncton, second-largest city of New Brunswick, with a population of twenty-two thousand. In the brightly lighted station square and grounds stood a solid mass of thirty thousand men, women, and children, with ten thousand more lining the tracks out of the city. From that mass of humanity rose long waves of cheering, as the royal flyer slowly glided to a halt. In a few minutes King George came down the steps with Queen Elizabeth. The Prime Minister presented to Their Majesties Mayor and Mrs. McMonagle, and the band of the New Brunswick Regiment played 'God Save the King'.

The National Anthem being concluded, the Queen handed to Mrs. Mc-Monagle a beautiful bouquet of flowers, which she asked to be given to the local hospitals. Then the royal party passed through a guard of honour of war veterans and moved to the flood-lit reception dais. The band's playing of 'O Canada' was drowned out by the din of the acclamations.

Touched by the enthusiasm of the welcome, the King and Queen moved to the front of the stand and waved to the crowd, who broke into still wilder acclamations, which caused the King to remark to Premier Dysart that Moncton's demonstration ranked among the finest night spectacles of the tour.

Amidst the acclaim, the children's parade began to march past the royal stand in order that all the children might see their King and Queen. Slowly the eight thousand boys and girls walked past in rows of ten, cheering and waving their flags. Realizing that this procession would take a long time, Mayor McMonagle decided to proceed with the official programme. Moving in front of the stand, he asked His Majesty to accept an address from the City of Moncton. Two little girls, Pauline Doiron and Joan Lockhart, came forward carrying a basket of flowers, which Mrs. McMonagle presented to the Queen. Then Mayor McMonagle introduced to Their Majesties a number of prominent citizens.

On their way back to the royal coach, the King and Queen passed in front of the guard of honour formed by ex-servicemen, and shook hands and chatted briefly with several of the veterans. After the Mayor had presented police and military officers, Their Majesties mounted the steps and stood on the flood-lit rear platform, waving to the crowd, as the train slowly pulled away.

About eleven o'clock, the train halted at Sackville to change locomotives. Five thousand people from Sackville, Amherst, Aulac, and other neighbouring points were tightly packed in and around the station. The town was brightly lighted and decorated. The stop was unscheduled, and the blinds were drawn in the royal coach at so late an hour. But the crowd refused to give up the chance of a lifetime. Cheers broke out, and cries of 'We want the King! We want the Queen!' For over five minutes the chant went on, and then the locomotive blew its whistle. Suddenly, as the train began slowly to move, the coach door opened and the King and Queen came out onto the observation platform. Wild acclamations roared in the night until the Sovereigns, waving to the bystanders, vanished in the distance.

The royal train now sped away on its thirty-five-mile run to Cape Tormentine. There it rested for the night on the shore of the Northumberland Strait opposite Prince Edward Island, the next province on the royal itinerary.

PRINCE EDWARD ISLAND

NEXT MORNING, Wednesday, June 14, rain poured down on the royal train, which had been shunted close to the wharf at Cape Tormentine, and on twenty thousand spectators assembled on both sides of the track. At 9:20 the train was backed from the pier until the royal coach was well beyond the head of the spectators' lines. After a while it slowly moved forward towards the pier again, with Their Majesties standing on the coach platform waving to the crowd, who cheered them with long, warm acclamations.

When the royal train had reached its place on the wharf, the Sovereigns entered their coach to get ready for the voyage across the Northumberland Strait. When they came out again, the Queen put out her hand to feel the rain and remarked to the King: 'It's raining as hard as it can.' The King, shrugging his shoulders, said: 'Well, let's go and make a dive for it.'

They entered the automobile waiting for them at the steps. Soon, however, they had to leave the car, about a hundred yards from the destroyer's mooring berth, because railway tracks blocked the way. They were therefore obliged to walk in the downpour. Thus were Their Majesties piped aboard H.M.C.S. *Skeena*, which at once hoisted the Royal Standard; for the first time a British Sovereign was to sail in a ship of the Canadian Navy.

Greeted at the gangway by Commander H. T. W. Grant, Their Majesties went below to remove their wet cloaks. Immediately the *Skeena*, accompanied by her sister ship the *Saguenay*, and flanked by police patrol boats, left the dock and began the crossing of the Strait. Overhead three Royal Canadian Air Force planes flew in formation, escorting the ship to Charlottetown.

During the two-and-a-half-hour crossing, the rain streamed steadily down, but half an hour before debarkation time the rain lifted, and the streets of Charlottetown dried quickly under a warm breeze.

The occasion of the royal visit had brought thirty-five thousand persons swarming into the capital, cramming all available space along the short royal

route from Marine Wharf to the Province Building. Red, white, and blue
bunting stretched across public buildings, store fronts displayed multi-
coloured banners, residences carried pennants and flags. The rain through the
night and morning had practically ruined the city's festive dress. Everything
was drenched: bunting, streamers, banners, and even flags hung limp and
lifeless. But nothing was able on such a day to dampen the enthusiasm of the
Islanders who crowded the streets in thousands along the procession route;
when the rain stopped half an hour before the royal arrival, thousands more
came out of houses, churches, and shops, where they had taken temporary
refuge.

At 12:25 the *Skeena* slipped alongside the Marine Wharf, while a royal
salute by the 8th Medium Battery, R.C.A., thundered from Victoria Park,
and tremendous cheers rose from the waiting throngs. Overhead the escorting
planes zoomed and circled gracefully, dipping low in a salute. A few minutes
later, Their Majesties appeared and walked down the gangplank. Instantly
the band played the National Anthem; then from the crowd massed on the
Marine Wharf a mighty acclaim burst forth, welcoming the Sovereigns.

Greeting Their Majesties ashore, Prime Minister King presented Lieutenant-
Governor George D. DeBlois and Mrs. DeBlois, Premier Thane A. Campbell
and Mrs. Campbell, Mayor E. A. Foster and Mrs. Foster.

The King first inspected the guard of honour formed by the Prince Edward
Island Highlanders. Then, amidst great acclamations from the crowded piers,
Their Majesties took their seats in their automobile. Preceded by a motor-
cycle escort of Mounties, the royal procession moved towards the city. Along
Great George Street Their Majesties rode between two solid lanes of shouting
citizens. The cheers turned into an ovation when the Sovereigns reached
Queen Square and the Province Building, where the greatest crowds of the
day were assembled.

Alighting at the carpeted steps of the historic stone building, which was
decorated in blue drapery and Union Jacks, Their Majesties were welcomed
by Premier and Mrs. Campbell, and proceeded up the stairs to the Confederation Chamber, where the other members of the provincial Cabinet awaited
their arrival. The smallest of the government reception chambers visited in
the royal tour was also the most interesting historically: in this room were
convened in 1864 the meetings that led to the formation of the Dominion of
Canada by the Fathers of Confederation.

Their Majesties took their places before the very table around which
the Confederation conference was held. Besides the royal party and the
government members, only a few persons were present in the small galleries.

Premier Campbell read the address of welcome to the King on behalf of the Government and people of Prince Edward Island. After accepting the illuminated address from the hands of the Premier, His Majesty gave him his written reply, in which he returned thanks for the sentiments expressed in the address and for the warm welcome of the Province.

Then Mayor Foster, wearing his gold chain of office, presented His Majesty with an address of welcome on behalf of the citizens of Charlottetown. The address mentioned the several historic connections between the royal family and the city, notably the successive visits of three sons of Queen Victoria to Charlottetown. It recalled the three days spent in the city by the King himself, as a midshipman on board H.M.S. *Cumberland*.

Their Majesties were then asked to sign the visitors' book. The King signed first, and then the Queen. The King, who stood at her side, pointed to the blank on the page where the date was to be written. The Queen looked up a little puzzled and asked: 'Is this the fourteenth?'—'What do you think it must be?' the King replied laughingly, 'Yesterday was the thirteenth, you know.'

In the meantime the crowds outside were chanting 'We want the King! We want the Queen!' Then, while the Sovereigns were signing the visitors' register, the bells of St. Dunstan's Basilica across the square began playing the National Anthem, and the children massed in front of the Province Building picked up the words.

After the ceremonies Their Majesties inspected the Confederation Chamber with great interest, looking at the tablets, shields, and inscriptions decorating the historic room. Then, led by Premier Campbell, Their Majesties proceeded to the balcony overlooking Parliament Square and its vast crowds of eager people. As the Sovereigns walked to the stone railing, the solid mass of spectators stretching in all directions roared an enthusiastic greeting. The scarlet-uniformed band of the Prince Edward Light Horse played the National Anthem. The music over, a tremendous acclaim swelled from the crowd.

Their Majesties emerged from the Province Building, entered their open car, and, preceded by police officers on motor-cycles, drove through the city's main streets towards Government House, between deep rows of enthusiastic spectators.

Arriving at Government House, King George and Queen Elizabeth were received on the porch by the Lieutenant-Governor and Mrs. DeBlois, who escorted them into the residence. After a brief period of rest, the sixty-five luncheon guests were presented to Their Majesties, and then the King and Queen entered the dining-room. During the luncheon the King told the

Lieutenant-Governor that Prince Edward Island looked very much like England, with its red cliffs and green meadows. He recalled his previous three days' visit to Charlottetown in 1913 as a midshipman, when he had refereed a cricket match between a Charlottetown eleven and a team from H.M.S. *Cumberland*, on which he was serving.

During the luncheon showers began once more to fall from a leaden sky. As a result the proposed garden party and outdoor reception that were to follow the Government luncheon had perforce to be abandoned. In the meantime more than five hundred guests invited to the garden party had assembled in the grounds, hoping for a let-up in the showers. Equal to any occasion, the King and Queen, heedless of the rain, went out into the garden to extend an informal greeting to the outside guests. They walked a short distance back and forth among them and were given an enthusiastic reception.

Their Majesties departed from the viceregal residence in their limousine with the hood up, for the rain was still coming down intermittently. Passing between two lines of war veterans drawn up along the driveway, the Sovereigns rode for their last tour through the city on their way to the Marine Wharf. All streets were again crammed by the Islanders, exhibiting contempt for the weather, which on this day, of all days, had so much belied the Island's reputation of no fog or rain. Although tinged with wistful regret at the bad weather, farewell acclamations were no less hearty than during the morning drive. Again Great George Street and the wharf roadway in particular were jammed with cheering bystanders. The acclaim never flagged for a moment from Government House to the Marine Wharf.

The royal car halted fifteen feet from the gangplank of the waiting destroyer *Skeena*, and the rushing crowd was stopped only a few feet away. Their Majesties alighted, and, smiling at the crowd, walked through the guard of honour of the Royal Canadian Navy Volunteer Reserve. After the Queen had shaken hands with the men of the motor-cycle escort, Their Majesties bade good-bye to their official hosts, the Lieutenant-Governor, the Premier, and the Mayor, and then boarded the *Skeena*, being met at the rail by Commander Grant. A royal salute of guns boomed in the distance; the warship cut loose and began to move away from the pier.

From the *Skeena*, slowly drawing away from the dock, the departure was an inspiring spectacle. Against the background of the city among its green trees, the three large piers jutting deep into the sea were covered with a solid mass of humanity waving flags, hats, and handkerchiefs, with great cheers of Godspeed. The King and Queen high on deck waved their friendly farewell to Prince Edward Island and slowly faded away in the distance.

Leaving Charlottetown at half past four, the *Skeena*, escorted by her sister ship *Saguenay* close astern, plunged through a rough sea and intermittent rain for the two hours and ten minutes required for the diagonal crossing of fifty miles from Prince Edward Island to Pictou.

NOVA SCOTIA

AT 6:40 THAT EVENING, King George and Queen Elizabeth entered the province of Nova Scotia, the ninth and last of the provinces visited by Their Majesties. A rainstorm that slashed the town of Pictou during the afternoon had failed to dim the enthusiasm of fifteen thousand spectators assembled in a town of three thousand inhabitants. The procession route was spanned by three beautiful arches of greenery with a Gaelic inscription of welcome. Early in the afternoon the people had begun to mass in front of the reception stand erected on the pier, while thousands gathered at vantage-points along the royal route. Before six o'clock the rain came to an end.

Entering the spacious harbour, the *Skeena* docked in a few minutes. The gangway was lowered and, coming up with a smile at the picturesque grouping of people on the wharf and the skirl of bagpipes filling the air, Their Majesties were piped over the side, and set foot for the first time on Nova Scotian soil. The Royal Standard fluttered from the flagpole, and a great wave of cheering rolled over the harbour. The massed bands played the National Anthem and the 83rd Field Battery, R.C.A., fired a royal salute.

At the entrance of the landing-pier already waited the official hosts of the day, Mayor Thomas R. Hooper and Mrs. Hooper, with the Honourable J. L. Ilsley, Nova Scotia's representative in the federal Cabinet, whom Prime Minister King presented to Their Majesties. Proceeding through the decorated shed, the King and Queen, emerging into view of the crowd, were greeted with thunderous cheers as they walked to the reception stand, in front of which was drawn up a detachment of soldiers with a group of veterans in the centre.

On the dais, Mayor Hooper presented His Majesty with an address of welcome and loyalty on behalf of the Corporation and citizens of Pictou.

The Mayor next presented prominent citizens of Pictou County, while the pipers played Scottish tunes.

The presentations over, Their Majesties walked to the ex-servicemen forming the guard of honour. Amidst a storm of applause and cheers, the King and Queen shook hands and chatted with the veterans.

About seven o'clock Their Majesties entered the royal limousine which had been brought to Pictou. As the car moved off, the massed spectators raised volleys of acclamations, and the guns on Battery Hill boomed out a royal salute.

The procession route, with its British and Scottish flags flying everywhere, was lined by war veterans, the Pictou Highlanders, and volunteer citizens from local organizations. Repeatedly waving to the spectators, Their Majesties were warmly acclaimed during the drive through the town, especially along Front Street, where an arch had been erected in honour of the Queen. Eight girls in Highland costume stood on graduated pedestals, four on each side, with a piper playing at the base. The arch bore the Gaelic inscription 'Failte Dhuibh Gu Albaim Nuadh' (Welcome to You to New Scotland). At Battery Hill Their Majesties were hailed lustily by a group of Micmac Indians wearing beaded buckskins and head-dresses of feathers.

To the accompaniment of a last burst of cheers, the royal automobile drove out of Pictou.

On the drive from Pictou to New Glasgow, eighteen miles south, the cars of the royal party sped along the highway until they reached Lyons Brook. Here the royal limousine slowed to a crawl, and Their Majesties were acclaimed by a massed crowd of one thousand children from thirty-three country schools.

Driving through wind and intermittent rain, the royal procession arrived at New Glasgow about eight o'clock. In spite of the weather, thousands had flocked in from all over the district, many coming by train and car from Cape Breton Island. War veterans from eight counties lined the streets. Girl Guides and Boy Scouts and members of various associations were massed at the station. Along the royal route were drawn up battalions of Highlanders, artillerymen, engineers, and cadets. There were more kilts to be seen in New Glasgow than in any town or city yet visited during the royal tour. Even the high school band wore kilts, as did the cadet corps. More than thirty thousand onlookers were cramming the streets all along the two-mile procession route.

Entering New Glasgow, the royal automobile was warmly and continuously acclaimed as it passed through cheering throngs. When it reached the station square and Their Majesties emerged, the eight thousand people jammed round the square gave them an ovation of cheers. Prime Minister King introduced Mayor N. D. Mason, who presented to His Majesty an illuminated address of loyalty and welcome on behalf of New Glasgow. He then presented a number of prominent citizens.

The official ceremony over, Their Majesties descended from the dais and walked over to the veterans, who immediately encircled the Sovereigns. Amidst outbursts of cheers the King and Queen, unmindful of the exhausting programme of the day, mingled with the ex-servicemen, shaking hands and chatting with a number of them. As Their Majesties mounted the steps of the royal coach for the last farewell, the spectators burst through the lines of the soldiers, Mounted Police, and special constables, and swarmed onto the platform beside the train, their cheers welling up as the King and Queen waved to them from the coach platform. The band played 'Will Ye No Come Back Again', and, as the royal train got under way, the National Anthem.

Next morning, June 15, the last day of the royal tour, a glorious sun brightened a cloudless blue sky. At 8:35 the blue train departed from Valley, under the gaze of admiring onlookers, en route for Halifax, a distance of sixty-eight miles. But first, four miles from Valley, it made a stop for servicing at Truro. When, at 8:40, the big locomotive slowly glided to a stop at the station, which was draped in bunting and flags, more than thirty thousand spectators stood waiting behind a double line of war veterans.

Waving to the cheering crowd, Their Majesties descended to the platform. They were greeted by the Governor General and the Lady Tweedsmuir, who had come to Truro from Halifax early in the morning to join the royal party. A fresh outburst of acclamations came from the crowd when the King and Queen walked along the platform, inspecting the war veterans, chatting and shaking hands with them, and so moving closer to the throngs at the other end of the station.

At 9:18 Their Majesties returned to the platform of their coach amidst a great ovation. As they waved a last farewell from the moving train, school children sang 'O Canada' and 'God Save the King'.

Through the Nova Scotian countryside the flyer steamed towards Halifax. All stations—especially Stewiacke and Shubenacadie—were bright with flags and filled with large crowds who cheered the royal train as it passed through.

Meanwhile, for the second time during the tour, a personal investiture was held on board the royal train. Between Truro and Bedford, in the royal coach, King George conferred the insignia of Knight Grand Cross of the Victorian Order on Lord Tweedsmuir. He also granted to Mr. Shuldham Redfern, the Governor General's secretary, the title of Knight Commander of the Victorian Order, and Lieutenant-Colonel Eric Mackenzie, Comptroller of Government House, was made Commander of the same Order. It was the first time that such a ceremony had been performed in Canada: the previous investiture had taken place in the United States.

The only halt between Truro and Halifax, a distance of sixty-four miles, occurred after passing the suburban village of Bedford, where a numerous throng had acclaimed the royal flyer. At the King's own request, a stop was made at Prince's Lodge so that a photograph could be taken of the members, Canadian and British, of the royal party. They all gathered at the rear of the royal coach, but the King decided otherwise, declaring 'Let us have the car's side as a background.' Turning to the government photographer, he said: 'Let us be placed according to size, the shorter ones in front.' Whereupon Commander Abel Smith said: 'Dr. Lanctot, step in front.'—'Yes,' the King added, 'quite right, next to me here.' Everybody being given his place, the photographer climbed upon a small railway tool shed and took several photographs of the group.

Then the King stood on the platform of his coach and turned his movie camera on the scenery round Prince's Lodge, which is the site of a residence built and occupied by the Duke of Kent, Queen Victoria's father, of which now remains only the wooden bandstand on a hilltop beside the water.

Skirting for six miles the beautiful shore of Bedford Basin, the great inner harbour of Halifax, the train now entered upon the last lap of the great continental tour, with Halifax the last Canadian city to be visited before embarking on the *Empress of Britain* en route to Newfoundland, London, and Buckingham Palace.

HALIFAX

OLDEST BRITISH CITY of the Dominion and capital of Nova Scotia, Halifax had declared the day of the visit of the King and Queen, June 15, a public holiday for the province and 'a day of general thanksgiving and rejoicing'.

The whole province seemed to have pilgrimaged to the capital. The influx was so great that on the previous night thousands were unable to secure any kind of accommodation. People had to sleep aboard boats in the harbour or in sleeping-coaches in railway yards. Many slept by spells in their automobiles, many crouched on benches or in doorways, and others spent the night walking the streets.

Next morning additional streams of humanity poured into the city. Towns, fishing villages, and rural districts were almost deserted by their populations. There were blue-bereted veterans from all the eighteen counties of the province. From Massachusetts and other New England states came hundreds of Americans. Groups of Micmac Indians could be seen in feathered head-dresses and beaded buckskins. Swarming in thousands, children had come from everywhere. Two boys had walked fourteen miles with nothing to eat but a bag of doughnuts.

At 12:05, as the royal train rolled into the decorated station, a twenty-one-gun salute crashed from Citadel Hill, and cheers broke out from all sections of the crowds surrounding the station. A minute later the King and Queen stepped down to the platform, saluted with an immense acclaim. Their Majesties were then welcomed by the Governor General and the Lady Tweedsmuir, heading the official host party. Prime Minister Mackenzie King presented to the Sovereigns the Lieutenant-Governor of Nova Scotia and Mrs. Irwin, Premier and Mrs. Macdonald, and the Mayor of Halifax and Mrs. Mitchell.

After the King had inspected the guard of honour formed by the Royal Canadian Regiment, the Sovereigns returned to the train, at the side of which its entire crew had been lined up. Both the King and the Queen shook hands with each of the personnel as they were presented individually by Dr. E. H. Coleman. Members of the Government House staff, two secretaries, and the only woman stenographer on board the royal train were also presented. The Sovereigns also shook hands with the eight Mounties forming the protective escort of the royal train. Later in the day the sixty-five persons thus presented received personal gifts—cigarette cases, tie pins, or cuff links—from the Sovereigns.

Passing through a narrow lane of applauding onlookers, Their Majesties proceeded to their automobile and headed the royal procession to Province House, driving through streets jammed with cheering people, at whom the King and Queen smiled and waved.

As the royal car rolled into the Province House Square with its dense mass of Boy Scouts, Girl Guides, and members of women's associations, the ovation increased until the Sovereigns disappeared into the building.

Escorted by Premier and Mrs. Macdonald, Their Majesties moved into the stately, high-ceilinged room, filled with distinguished guests. The Sergeant-at-arms, dressed in the dark-green Macleod tartan, brought forward the mace, and the King, after lightly touching the golden crown, took his place on the dais with the Queen.

Premier Macdonald read an address to His Majesty from the people of Nova Scotia. The King then handed to the Premier his reply in writing. The Queen was presented with a bouquet of red roses by eight-year-old Colinne Macdonald, the Premier's daughter. Then Premier Macdonald introduced to Their Majesties the members of the provincial Cabinet.

Led by the Premier, the King, accompanied by the Queen, next moved to a flag-draped painting. As His Majesty pulled the silken cord, the Union Jack swept back, unveiling a fine portrait of the late King, George V. The artist, Sir Wyly Grier, was presented to Their Majesties.

Leaving Province House in the midst of a rousing ovation from the multitude occupying every foot of space, Their Majesties drove again through the city on solid waves of cheering, only to stop in front of the City Hall, where a special section was occupied by war veterans, nursing sisters, and one hundred and fifty mothers who had lost sons in the Great War.

On a high reception platform draped with bunting in front of the City Hall, Their Majesties were greeted by Mayor and Mrs. Mitchell. The Mayor presented the King with an address of welcome on behalf of the citizens of Halifax, and Mrs. M. T. Sullivan, the first woman alderman to enter the City Council, offered to the Queen a bouquet of orchids and a sprig of Scottish heather. Mayor Mitchell then presented to the Sovereigns members of the City Council and their wives as well as senior civic officials and their wives. The ceremony concluded with the King and Queen's signing of the city's Golden Book.

Departing from the City Hall, Their Majesties proceeded to the Nova Scotian Hotel for the luncheon given by the Government of Nova Scotia.

In the large banquet hall, resplendent with golden linen and roses, two hundred guests, leaders in Nova Scotia's life and their wives, had already taken their places when Their Majesties walked in, escorted by Premier and Mrs. Macdonald.

At coffee time, the King having knocked with the gavel, silence fell, and Premier Macdonald rose and proposed the health of the King. The orchestra played the National Anthem, and the toast was drunk. The Premier then proposed the toast to the Queen, which was also duly honoured.

Rising again, the Premier said:

Your Majesties, Ladies and Gentlemen:

This is a day of great significance and of deep emotion for every Britisher. It marks the end of Their Majesties' visit to Canada and the United States—a journey that, in its conception, in its circumstances, and, I believe too, in its results, has had no parallel in the long history of our people. The occasion, most memorable in itself, will be made still more impressive, I am sure, by the speech which His Majesty has graciously consented to deliver here.

I am most happy to announce that immediately on the conclusion of His Majesty's address Her Majesty the Queen will say a word of farewell to the people of Canada.

And now, Ladies and Gentlemen, His Majesty the King.

As His Majesty rose, the company broke into prolonged applause. The King spoke in English and French with moving earnestness.

The time has come for the Queen and myself to say good-bye to the people of Canada.

You have given us a welcome of which the memory will always be dear to us. In our travels across your great country, we have seen not a little of its infinite variety of natural wealth and natural beauty. We have had the privilege of meeting Canadians, old and young, of many proud racial origins and in all walks of life. We hope we have made many friends among you.

We have had the opportunity, also, of crossing your border and paying an all too brief visit to Canada's great and friendly neighbour to the south. Our minds and hearts are full. We leave your shores after some of the most inspiring and illuminating weeks in our lives.

Mon premier devoir est de vous remercier du fond de mon coeur. C'est grâce à vous qu'il nous a été permis de voir tant de choses en peu de temps. Nous avons a vous remercier, non seulement des égards d'ordre personnel que vous avez bien voulu nous témoigner mais également des soins minutieux apportés à tous les détails de notre réception. Je dois dire que nous venons s'accomplir presqu'un miracle en surmontant les nombreuses difficultés que présente le parcours d'espaces si vastes en un temps aussi limité.

I return to England with a new sense of the resources and of the responsibilities of our British Empire. I am confident that Canada has before her a development far beyond the most optimistic dreams of her pioneers. Her growth in material wealth is fully assured. For her sons and daughters, I wish her an even greater growth in the stature of mind and spirit.

I go home with another thought, which is a comfort and an inspiration. From the Atlantic to the Pacific, and from the tropics to the Arctic, lies a large part of the earth where there is no possibility of war between neighbours, whose peoples are wholly dedicated to the pursuits of peace, a pattern to all men of how civilized nations should live together. It is good to know that such a region exists, for what man can do once he can do again. By God's grace yours may yet be the example which all the world will follow.

The King sat down, and the audience burst into warm applause. Then the Queen was introduced by Premier Macdonald: 'Ladies and Gentlemen, Her Majesty the Queen.'

Long applause greeted Her Majesty. She delivered her farewell message in a clear, mellow voice, with a tinge of subdued emotion.

I cannot leave Canada without saying a word of farewell to you all, and thanking you for the wealth of affection that you have offered us throughout these unforgettable weeks.

Seeing this country, with all its varied beauty and interest, has been a real delight to me; but what has warmed my heart in a way I cannot express in words is the proof you have given us everywhere that you were glad to see us. And in return, I want particularly to tell the women and children of Canada how glad I am to have seen so many of them. Some, I know, came scores of miles to meet us, and that has touched me deeply. There were others, I fear, whom distance, or illness, prevented from coming: to these I should like to send a special word of greeting—they have been always in my thoughts.

This wonderful tour of ours has given me memories that the passage of time will never dim. To the people of Canada and to all the kind people in the United States who welcomed us so warmly last week—to one and all on this great friendly continent, I say: Thank you. God be with you and God bless you. Au revoir et Dieu vous bénisse.

The Queen resumed her seat amidst great applause, and a few minutes later the whole company rose for the National Anthem, which brought the luncheon to an end.

From the dining-room Their Majesties, led by Premier and Mrs. Macdonald, moved into the foyer where a number of guests not previously introduced were presented.

The presentations over, the Sovereigns graciously consented to appear on a balcony of the hotel. In the street and grounds below stretched on all sides a moving sea of spectators. The moment Their Majesties stepped into full view, cheers rose up from all sections of the vast assemblage, while the King and Queen waved to the crowds.

At half past three Their Majesties left the Nova Scotian for their longest drive through the city. For more than half an hour, preceded by the motorcycle escort of red-coated Mounties, they rode triumphantly along miles of streets thronged with cheering citizens.

A few minutes later the royal limousine halted at Camp Hill Military Hospital. To the cheers of several hundred war veterans and their families assembled in the spacious grounds, the Sovereigns were greeted by Dr. M. A. Macaulay, who presented the hospital staff and nurses. The King and Queen walked on the lawns along a row of twelve cot cases, speaking a few words to each of them. This unscheduled stop was made at the King's own request.

From the hospital, the royal parade proceeded along Summer and Sackville Streets to the Garrison Grounds for the last official ceremony of the day: a pageant of the Scottish founding of Nova Scotia. Here the spectacle was unique, and undoubtedly one of the grandest and most impressive of the whole tour.

On the side of Citadel Hill, which slopes gently up from the Garrison Grounds, were ranged, facing the royal dais, twenty thousand school children with small flags in their hands. Surrounding them and stretching in all directions were massed some forty thousand men and women. When Their Majesties, accompanied by Lieutenant-Governor and Mrs. Irwin, Prime Minister Mackenzie King, and Premier and Mrs. Macdonald, stepped out of their car and walked into full view, a solid hillside of tightly-packed humanity raised its voice in a chorus of acclaim.

Amidst this scene Their Majesties moved along the red-carpeted boardwalk leading to the royal dais, where they took their places. After a massed choir of six hundred boys and girls had sung 'O Canada' and the Queen's favourite song, 'Over the Sea to Skye', the historical pageant was presented. In three scenes, against the stage background of Edinburgh Castle, it depicted the granting of Nova Scotia's territory to Sir William Alexander, the return of the exploring party from North America, and finally the issuing of the colony's royal charter in 1621.

As the Sovereigns stepped from the dais after the pageant, Chief Louis Paul of the Shubenacadie Indians presented the King with two tiny birch-bark canoes for Princesses Elizabeth and Margaret Rose.

As Their Majesties withdrew with the royal party, one section of the crowd shattered the police lines and in a quick rush pressed along the boardwalk as King George and Queen Elizabeth proceeded towards the Public Gardens. As the Sovereigns were about to reach the gate, another throng surged forward across Bell Road and Sackville Street. In a minute it appeared that the King and Queen would be engulfed by the two converging onrushes, but the people halted spontaneously, enclosing in a small circle the friendly Sovereigns, who, quite undismayed, stopped to say a few words to several elderly ladies in the crowd. With a last smile to all, the Sovereigns emerged from the throng and entered the gate of the Public Gardens.

Their Majesties strolled through the beautiful gardens famed for their many fine trees and artistic flower beds. The King consented to replant a small English oak, which had grown in Point Pleasant Park from an acorn brought over from Windsor Castle. First planted on the day of the King's Coronation, it was now almost four feet high, and the King could not refrain from a bit of wonder at such a growth.

Coming out of the Public Gardens gate at the corner of South Park Street and Spring Garden Road, Their Majesties resumed their drive through the city. After traversing the grounds of Dalhousie University, the royal limousine entered the hospital zone, and here prevailed a tense hush of expectancy. In front of the Children's Hospital, tiny cots and chairs had been placed on the lawn for young patients, waving small Union Jacks. Their Majesties ordered the car stopped, and four-year-old Marguerite Davis was lifted by a nurse to present a bouquet of carnations and roses to the Queen.

In completing the city tour, Their Majesties proceeded through streets lined with cheering crowds to Government House where, about half past five, they were received at the entrance by Lieutenant-Governor and Mrs. Irwin. The King and Queen were entertained at a farewell tea, which was also attended by members of the royal party.

At 6:12, when Their Majesties came out for the short drive to the docks and the *Empress of Britain*, they walked over to the four Mounties, Sergeant H. W. H. Williams, and Constables J. A. L. S. Langlois, J. C. Coughlin, and R. Portelance, who had acted throughout the tour as their personal orderlies. The King and Queen shook hands with each of them, expressing thanks for their services, and posed with them for a photograph.

Then Their Majesties drove to the Ocean Terminal, where stood a mass of cheering people. After the band had played the National Anthem, the King inspected a guard of honour from the *Fundy* and the *Gaspé*, Canadian mine-sweepers. Then, amidst a storm of cheers, Their Majesties walked up the ramp to the pier. They stopped to chat for a few minutes with their Nova Scotia official hosts.

Followed by the royal suite, the Sovereigns moved into the shed, in which hundreds of veterans had been assigned the honour of lining the red carpet leading to the ship. As the Sovereigns vanished into the building, excited spectators broke through the lines for the fifth time that day, and hundreds of them pushed their way into the huge building, constantly pressing forward to get closer to the royal couple. Arm-locked veterans struggled to keep a path clear for Their Majesties and the royal suite. Perfectly at ease, the King and Queen seemed to enjoy the enthusiastic scene. Anxious also to meet the veterans, they walked to the nearest men and began chatting and mingling with them.

Their Majesties had now reached the carpeted gangway. Before stepping aboard the *Empress of Britain*, both the King and the Queen, half turning to the crowd and the veterans, waved a cheerful farewell, which was answered with a gale of cheers; the guns of a royal salute boomed in the distance.

A few minutes later the members of the press who had accompanied Their Majesties through Canada and into the United States were invited on board the liner. They lined up in a circle on an upper deck, and, with no introduction, the King and Queen went round the group shaking hands and chatting with everyone. When a reporter suggested to the King that he must be rather tired, His Majesty replied: 'No, but you must be. I really think you have had a harder job than we have.' On taking leave of the group, the King said: 'Thank you so much for what you have done. We will remember you with gratitude.'

The Sovereigns descended to the ship's library. The King sent for the President of the Canadian National Railways, S. J. Hungerford, and expressed to him his appreciation of the excellence of the railway service during the long journey over the Company's lines. Then Canadian members of the royal entourage were received individually for a last farewell from the King and Queen.

Finally King George and Queen Elizabeth had a farewell chat with Prime Minister Mackenzie King, asking him to express to Canada their warmest gratitude for the country's invitation and the wonderful, heartfelt reception extended to them by all the people. As a memento of the historic visit, Their Majesties presented the Prime Minister with a large scarlet-bound volume entitled 'Records of the Past'. Then, last of all to voice Canada's good-bye, the Governor General and the Lady Tweedsmuir took leave of the King and Queen.

At 7:18 the King and Queen suddenly appeared on the bridge, a hundred feet up, and waved to the thousands of people in sight. All over the docks roars of acclamation broke out again and again, with the waving of hats, berets, and flags. For about five minutes, the smiling Sovereigns waved to their people amidst gales of cheers.

Then Their Majesties disappeared from view. At 7:32 the big liner began to swing away from the pier. Warm acclaims rose from hearts and throats, and presently the King and Queen were back on the bridge, waving to the crowd.

The royal procession formed and headed out to sea, with the Canadian destroyers *Skeena* and *Saguenay* leading the way in a single line ahead. Then, flying the Royal Standard, came the stately *Empress of Britain*, and close in line followed, one astern of the other, the two British cruisers *Glasgow* and *Southampton*; overhead flew in perfect formation three great fighting sea-planes. In the harbour, three or four score of yachts, schooners, and motor-boats, all dressed with flags, in company with the *Bluenose*, racing champion of sailing-ships, let go their whistles and fog-horns in a boisterous salute.

High above the city, the slopes of Citadel Hill were black and teeming with people. All along the piers and the whole waterfront were gathered about one hundred thousand men, women, and children. They cheered and waved as the great white liner glided by with the King and Queen standing on the bridge waving farewell to Canada.

At a given signal a massed choir of one thousand voices, stationed on the breakwater, off the Royal Nova Scotia Yacht Squadron, sang 'Auld Lang Syne', followed by 'Will Ye No Come Back Again'. Then the words of 'God Save the King' soared towards the royal yacht.

Then in the gathering dusk great red flames leaped skywards from an immense bonfire on the heights of Chebucto Head, lighting, like a gigantic torch, Their Majesties' way home.

EMPRESS OF BRITAIN

AFTER LEAVING HALIFAX, the King and Queen remained on the bridge of the *Empress of Britain* for nearly an hour before turning in. Escorted by the British *Southampton* and *Glasgow*, the royal liner ploughed ahead at twenty-four knots on her way to Newfoundland.

The King's desk was literally covered with farewell telegrams, wishing Their Majesties Godspeed and *bon voyage*. They had been sent by Lieutenant-Governors, Premiers, Mayors, and various institutions. The one message that stood out for its significance and deep cordiality came from Washington and the White House. President Roosevelt's telegram, dated June 15, read as follows:

> I cannot allow you and the Queen to sail for home without expressing once more the extreme pleasure which your all-too-brief visit to the United States gave us. The warmth of the welcome accorded you everywhere you visited in this country was the spontaneous outpouring of Americans who were deeply touched by the tact, the graciousness and the understanding hearts of our guests. I shall always like to think that you felt the sincerity of this manifestation of the friendship of the American people. Mrs. Roosevelt joins me in parting felicitations to Your Majesties and best wishes for a safe and pleasant voyage.

The same evening several letters dated June 15 and signed by the King on board the royal train before reaching Halifax were on their way to Cabinet Ministers, conveying Their Majesties' thanks to the various agencies that had contributed to the great success of the royal visit. Undoubtedly foremost in the King's mind was the following message of appreciation and thanks for the part played by the veterans during the royal tour, which was sent to the Minister of Pensions, the Honourable C. G. Power:

> *One of the most notable features of my Canadian tour has been the appearance everywhere of large and well-organized detachments of Veterans. It has always been a pleasure to me to see them, not only because of the particularly friendly character of their welcome, but also because their presence has given me some opportunity of showing my high appreciation of their past services to their country.*
>
> *I know well that the ideals that inspired them twenty years ago are still theirs, and that this fine body of men has never lost that sense of comradeship and of service to the common good which was perhaps the happiest legacy of the Great War.*
>
> *The Queen and I send them our best wishes, and our sincere thanks for the very valuable work they did throughout Canada in connection with our visit.*

To the Minister of National Defence, the Honourable Ian Mackenzie, came this letter congratulating and thanking the naval, military, and air forces for their services in the course of the royal visit:

> *Before we leave you today I wish to congratulate you very sincerely on the defence forces of the Dominion. Time has not permitted me to assist at the training exercises which are the only test of defence that*

peaceful conditions can provide. Our contact has, of necessity, been one of ceremonial. Even so, it has been easy to detect among all ranks that spirit of discipline and keenness to serve, without which the most thorough training would be useless.

In both oceans the Canadian Navy has been our escort, and on land as well there has been ample opportunity to see the smart efficiency of all ranks. Not only at Victoria, where I presented colours to the regular force, but repeatedly along our route where we have been greeted by detachments of the Naval Volunteer Reserve, have I been proud to notice that the same high standard has been maintained.

With the Army, too, both permanent and non-permanent militia, I have been deeply impressed. Wherever we have passed, escorts have been provided and streets have been lined by regular troops and by men who are prepared to devote a generous proportion of their spare time to the military service of their country. In every case their bearing has done the greatest credit to the uniform which they wear.

I regret that time has prevented me from seeing more of the Air Force. Faultless escorts I have seen, and on more than one occasion airmen and Air Force bands have contributed, second to none, to the pageantry of the streets. I am confident that the Air Force, though the youngest of the services, has already established a tradition no less brilliant than that of the senior branches, and that before it, associated with the air development of this vast land, lies a great and vital future.

As head of the three services I send my congratulations and thanks to all. Since the day on which the Queen and I first sailed into Canadian waters they have contributed in no small measure to the success and interest of our progress. I am proud to have made their close acquaintance.

A third message was received by Dr. E. H. Coleman, as Chairman of the Interdepartmental Committee, which supervised all arrangements and programmes of the royal tour. It read as follows:

During the last few weeks, I have had a better opportunity than anybody, perhaps, of seeing the results of the work that you and your colleagues have done in connection with my visit to Canada. I can appreciate, too, that your task began many months ago and that ever since the visit was first projected you have all been kept extremely busy by the preliminary arrangements.

The unqualified success of the tour must be a source of well-

deserved satisfaction to you and to the Civil Service of Canada generally. I want, however, to add my personal and most sincere thanks not only to the members of your committee and its sub-committees, but also to all the government departments concerned, and to all the provincial governments, and municipal authorities, without whose co-operation so comprehensive a tour of the Dominion could never have been made.

To the Prime Minister, the King had personally addressed two letters. The first commended the railways in the following terms:

My dear Prime Minister:

The Queen and I have travelled several thousands of miles, by land and by water, since we arrived in Canada. Our long journey has now been accomplished successfully, and with a regard for our comfort and for the demands of our timetable that calls for the highest praise. I know very well that this result could not have been achieved without an elaborate organization and the loyal and efficient co-operation of all connected with the great transportation systems of Canada.

On the railroads, and at sea, we have had the opportunity of meeting and talking with many of those who, in one capacity or another, were concerned with our journey; there are many others, however, with whom we have not been thus in contact.

I should be much obliged if you would make it known how grateful we are to all those engaged in this important department of Canada's national life for the great service they have rendered to us.

The second royal letter to Prime Minister King congratulated the police in the following terms:

My dear Prime Minister:

Through my long journey across Canada and back, I have been greatly impressed by the manner in which the police have carried out their duties.

These duties have not been easy; they have involved the handling of very large crowds, many of whom were women and children, and the constant supervision of the route along which I travelled. Their execution had called for a great deal of hard work, and the constant exercise of tact and discretion. On no occasion, however, have the police failed to perform them with the highest degree of efficiency.

I should be grateful, therefore, if you would kindly convey to the

members of all the various police forces concerned my hearty congra-
tulations on their efforts during the past few weeks, and the sincere
thanks of the Queen and myself for all that they have done for us.

I wish, too, to take this opportunity of paying a high tribute to
the members of many voluntary organizations, whose helpful col-
laboration on all occasions must have been invaluable to the officials
responsible for the local arrangements.

The last message from the royal pen went to the Governor General as
Chief Scout for Canada, for the Boy Scouts Association:

One of the pleasantest features of my tour through Canada has
been the sight of the strong contingents of Boy Scouts and Wolf Cubs
in all parts of the Dominion. I have been greatly struck not only by
their numbers, but by their smart appearance and fine physique. These
boys are indeed a credit to Canada and to the Boy Scout movement,
the value of which both you and I know so well.

As Chief Scout for Canada will you please convey to all members
of the Association my warm thanks for the good work they have
done in connection with my visit and my congratulations on the way
in which they are maintaining the Scout tradition in this great coun-
try. I wish them all the best of luck.

The *Empress of Britain* with her forty-two thousand tons differed vastly
from the twenty-one-thousand-ton *Empress of Australia*, which had brought
the Sovereigns to Canada. Twice the size of the other, she seemed all the
more enormous now because she carried as passengers only the sixteen
members of the royal party. Indeed, one had to find his way about the big
ship, which had eleven lounges and dining-rooms. On the first evening out,
as the King stepped out of the lift into the main lobby, from which led so
many doors, he was heard to remark with a smile: 'And now, where do we
go from here?'

The next day, near Cape Race, the *Berwick*, flagship of the Royal Navy's
America and West Indies Squadron, joined the royal flotilla. As she steamed
by with her band playing the National Anthem, the King took the salute
while standing on the bridge with the Queen. At half past six, the *Empress*
and her escort dropped anchor in Conception Bay on the east coast of Newfoundland, instead of proceeding to St. John's, for owing to her size the
Empress could not safely enter the land-locked harbour of the capital city.

Next morning, from the *Empress*, a last message to Canada was sent by the King addressed to the Governor General, Lord Tweedsmuir:

> From all parts of Canada messages bidding us farewell and wishing us godspeed have reached the Queen and myself on board the *Empress of Britain*.
>
> Their number is so great that we cannot hope to reply to them individually. Will you please ask each Lieutenant-Governor if he will kindly let it be known in his province how deeply grateful we are for these further proofs of Canada's affectionate goodwill toward us.

NEWFOUNDLAND

F OR THEIR MAJESTIES' last day in North America—Saturday, June 17—the Empire's oldest colony, Newfoundland, provided a triumphant close of the royal tour.

At daybreak the weather was not auspicious. Morning mists turned into a drizzle at Holyrood, the landing port. The picturesque village was gaily dressed in red, white, and blue bunting. Out in the harbour eight schooners of the Coasters' and Seamen's Associations formed the guard of honour.

About 9:10 the Governor, Sir Humphrey Walwyn, and Lady Walwyn arrived at the landing-stage, where already had assembled the six Commissioners who, since 1933, had administered the Island under the Governor.

Five minutes later a boat came from the *Berwick* and took the Governor, with his private secretary, Captain Schwartz, on board the royal yacht, which was anchored outside the harbour. The Governor welcomed the King and Queen on behalf of the Government and people of Newfoundland.

Just after ten o'clock, in a drizzling rain, Their Majesties boarded a blue naval barge, which headed across Conception Bay towards the shore, while a royal salute was fired from the escorting cruisers *Southampton* and *Glasgow*. As the royal barge neared the wharf, a great cheer rose from the spectators on the shore.

King George, accompanied by his equerry, Commander Abel Smith, and

Queen Elizabeth, accompanied by her ladies-in-waiting, Lady Nunburnholme and Lady Katharine Seymour, set foot on Newfoundland soil amid outbursts of cheering. The guard of honour formed by the Newfoundland Constabulary and the Newfoundland Rangers Force presented arms, and the band played the National Anthem.

The Governor and Lady Walwyn welcomed Their Majesties. Then the Governor presented the Honourable Commissioners administering Newfoundland. After the presentations, nine-year-old Christian Beuron presented the Queen with a bouquet of red and white carnations. Next, attended by the Governor, King George inspected the guard of honour. The inspection being completed, Their Majesties moved up the wharf towards the royal car.

Preceded by a police car and followed by eight automobiles carrying the members of the royal party and the Commissioners and their wives, the royal procession moved on amid tumultuous acclamations. Along the road from Holyrood to St. John's, it passed under twenty-one arches of welcome made of green spruce and decked with flags.

At half past eleven, the royal procession entered St. John's, the capital of the island. The city was gaily decorated: several beautiful arches of greenery spanned the streets. From early morning, people had been assembling at the junction of Hamilton Avenue and LeMarchant Road, where stood the city's reception pavilion. A light drizzle failed to lessen the eagerness of the crowds.

Preceded by a squad of motor-cycle police, and emerging from the city's large arch, the royal car was instantly greeted with tumultuous and ringing cheers. A few moments later, the King and Queen stepped from their car, and a shout of welcome welled from the multitude and soared again when Their Majesties smiled and acknowledged the ovation. The band played the National Anthem, and the King stood at the salute.

Greeted by the Governor, who presented the Mayor and Mrs. Carnell, Their Majesties took their places on the reception platform. Then Mayor Carnell read an address of welcome on behalf of the citizens of St. John's. The reading completed, Mayor Carnell handed to the King a silver casket containing the address, and then presented the city councillors and their wives.

After the presentations, the Governor led Their Majesties to the covered section of the pavilion, where a microphone had been installed. Then the King broadcast a message to the people of Newfoundland:

> It is a great pleasure to me to find myself once again in the capital city of this, the oldest colony in my Empire, where the Queen and I have been

deeply touched by the warmth of the welcome given us on all sides from the moment we set foot on shore at Holyrood.

I still cherish the happy memories of my last visit to the Island in 1913, when I was a cadet aboard H.M.S. *Cumberland*, and I have never forgotten the kindness and hospitality which I then received at your hands.

It is with deep feeling that I refer to the part played by Newfoundland in the Great War, the exploits of the Royal Newfoundland Regiment and the splendid work of members of the Newfoundland Royal Naval Reserve during the war, which have a proud place among the annals of Empire.

I well know that in recent years Newfoundland, like other parts of the world, has suffered from a period of severe economic stress, but the qualities of courage and endurance which have never failed the people of this country in the past will, I am confident, enable them once more to surmount their difficulties.

I am glad indeed to have this opportunity of expressing to all my subjects throughout the length and breadth of the Island and also those in Labrador my personal interest in their welfare, my deep sympathy with them in the trials which they have had to face, and my appreciation of their loyalty.

May God grant us all peace and prosperity.

Immediately following the broadcast, Their Majesties moved from the pavilion, and a gale of cheers swept over the multitude, resounding louder when the King and Queen, having entered their car, responded with a wave of the hand to the ovation. As they drove along the streets, cheer after cheer arose from the spectators.

At Garrison Hill an escort of mounted police joined in and rode ahead of the royal procession. A great outburst of acclamations from a massed throng climaxed the drive as the royal car entered the western gate of Government House. Immediately the Royal Standard broke from the flagpole. For the first time in history a British Sovereign was taking up residence in Newfoundland.

At the entrance to the historic residence was a colour party of war veterans bearing the Colour of the former Royal Newfoundland Regiment. The King saluted as the Colour was dipped and the band struck up the National Anthem. The King then inspected the guard of honour. When passing down the rear rank, the Governor presented to His Majesty Sergeant Thomas Rickett, the Empire's youngest recipient of the Victoria Cross, won at the age of seventeen during the Great War.

When the inspection was over, the Sovereigns entered Government House with the Governor and Lady Walwyn.

At half past twelve Their Majesties re-entered their car for the ceremony at the War Memorial. Acclaimed all along the route, the royal automobile halted near the arch of Trinity South. Cheered by the largest concourse of people ever seen in St. John's, the King and Queen walked through the ranks of ex-servicemen lined up on Water Street opposite the War Memorial.

When Their Majesties reached the base of the fine monument to Newfoundland's war dead with its bronze figure of a naval man and a soldier, the King laid a wreath of red and white carnations—inscribed 'From George, R.I., and Elizabeth, R.'—at the base of the Memorial. Stepping back three paces, he stood at attention a brief moment and then saluted.

Descending the steps of the Memorial amidst acclamations, the royal party was greeted by Mayor Carnell and escorted to the lawn, where the King, using a silver spade, planted a red oak tree, and the Queen planted another from England. The engraved silver spades were presented to Their Majesties.

The Sovereigns now returned to Water Street and, passing in front of the war veterans, both the King and the Queen halted to shake hands with some of the ex-soldiers and sailors and to talk with them. The Sovereigns then reentered their automobile for the drive through the city.

At half past one the Sovereigns took luncheon with the Governor and Lady Walwyn and the members of the royal entourage. After luncheon, the King and the Queen went out into the garden to pose for an official photograph.

In the meantime, more than a thousand guests had assembled in the grounds of Government House for the garden party given by the Governor and Lady Walwyn in honour of Their Majesties. Nearly two hundred of the guests had been invited to attend punctually at three o'clock for presentation to Their Majesties. These privileged ones were ushered into the drawing-room, where the presentations took place. They then went out to join the other guests in the gardens.

About half past three Their Majesties appeared at the head of the steps leading to the gardens. They walked between the lines of guests drawn up on both sides of the pathways. Accompanied by the Governor and Lady Walwyn, the King and Queen passed along, stopping every now and then to shake hands and talk with some of the men and women. At the Royal Pavilion in the centre of the grounds, the Governor presented to Their Majesties a number of prominent citizens.

Then took place the event of the day, an investiture of knighthood. It was conferred on the Honourable J. C. Puddester, Vice-Chairman of Newfoundland's Ruling Commission, who had been in the previous honours list. Four minor decorations were also conferred.

The investitures completed, Their Majesties left the pavilion and walked back through the lines of guests towards Government House. Inside Government House the King invested the Governor with the insignia of Knight Commander of St. Michael and St. George, and conferred the honour of Commander of the Victorian Order on Captain C.M.R. Schwartz, the Governor's private secretary.

At 5:05, accompanied by the Governor and Lady Walwyn in a second car, Their Majesties departed from Government House. Along the route dense crowds voiced a clamorous farewell to the Sovereigns.

At quarter past five, the royal car rolled into the Feildian Grounds for the last event of the royal visit before the sailing from Portugal Cove. There, round the track, were drawn up nearly three thousand of the Church Lads Brigade, Boy Scouts, and Girl Guides. Just after Their Majesties entered the grounds, the band struck up the National Anthem, and the royal automobile, moving slowly round the track, was acclaimed in a great ovation. Coming out of the grounds, the royal car drove up Robinson's Hill amid a continuous wave of cheers.

From St. John's to Portugal Cove, the more northern port also on Conception Bay, the nine-mile drive followed a winding road through a thinly-populated wilderness of rocky hills and green spruce. At quarter to six the royal procession drove into view of Portugal Cove, a fishing village, where two thousand men, women, and children lined the roadside. On the wharf Their Majesties received a royal salute from the guard of honour. Then Their Majesties bade farewell to the Honourable Commissioners and their wives, shaking hands and exchanging a few words with them, after which the Governor presented a few notables of Portugal Cove and Bell Island.

Then the King nodded to the Queen, and together they walked over to the veterans. They shook hands with scores of fishermen and miners, and chatted with a number of them.

After a final good-bye to the Governor and Lady Walwyn, Their Majesties proceeded on board the ferry-boat *Maneco*, which proudly hoisted the Royal Standard. As she moved off, with the King and Queen standing upon the deck and waving a last farewell, great acclaim rose from the shore, while in the distance the *Glasgow* fired a royal salute of twenty-one guns.

NEWFOUNDLAND–LONDON

LEAVING NEWFOUNDLAND'S SHORE with Their Majesties on board, the *Maneco* proceeded towards the *Glasgow*, which was lying two miles out from Portugal Cove. Once the royal party was on board the *Glasgow*, she steamed down the bay to the warships. Their Majesties proceeded to the ward room, where the officers were presented, and King George invested Captain C. Coltarb with the insignia of a Commander of the Victorian Order. Then the royal party returned to the waiting launch, which ploughed its way over to the *Southampton*. On board the cruiser the King conferred on Vice-Admiral G. F. B. Edward Collins the insignia of a Knight Commander of the Victorian Order, and on Captain F. W. Jeans the insignia of a Commander of the Victorian Order. Then once more the royal party descended to the launch, and this time it crossed over to the *Berwick*. Here the King conferred on Vice-Admiral Sir Sydney Meyrick, in his own cabin, the insignia of a Knight Commander of the Victorian Order.

Their Majesties were then taken in the pinnace to the *Empress of Britain*, which they boarded after eight o'clock. At half past eight, the royal flotilla weighed anchor.

Sunday, June 18, was a day of welcome rest on board the royal yacht. In the morning Their Majesties attended a sung service of the Church of England in the ship's main lounge, and in the evening entertained at dinner the commander of the *Empress*, Captain C. H. Sapsworth.

Before dinner on Monday, Queen Elizabeth spoke by transatlantic telephone from her drawing-room to Princess Elizabeth and Princess Margaret Rose.

Wednesday, June 21, was a busy day, with everybody packing on the eve of debarkation. On Thursday, mist and rain prevailed so steadily that the projected naval and air welcome by warships of the British fleet and aeroplanes of the Royal Air Force was regretfully cancelled by the King.

Shortly before noon, the King invested Captain Sapsworth, Surgeon Captain J. A. Maxwell, and Paymaster Captain L. A. daC. Ricci with the insignia of a Commander of the Victorian Order, and conferred the rank of Member of the Victorian Order on Lieutenant-Commander Peter Dawney. The King also presented personal gifts to several officers of the ship and others who had accompanied the Sovereigns during the voyage.

A few minutes later, in Yarmouth Roads, the destroyer *Kempenfelt* from Portsmouth ran alongside the royal liner. On board were Princess Elizabeth and Princess Margaret Rose, and, hopping with joy, the Princesses transferred at 12:20, to be met at the rail by the King and Queen. With cries of 'Hullo, Mummy', the Princesses hugged and kissed the Queen, and then the King.

Slowly the great white ship, with the King, Queen, and Princesses visible on the bridge, glided across to the dock, which was packed with people hailing her approach with continuous acclamations. On the landing-stage stood Queen Mary, accompanied by the Duke and Duchess of Gloucester, the Duke and Duchess of Kent, and the Princess Royal and the Earl of Harewood.

At 2:40 the royal yacht docked. Queen Mary and the members of her party went aboard, being met by the King and Queen on the promenade deck. Forty minutes later, the King, followed by the Queen with Princess Margaret Rose, and Queen Mary with Princess Elizabeth, walked ashore to a great chorus of acclamations.

On the pier Their Majesties were received by Lord Mottistone, Lord Lieutenant of Hampshire. The royal party then stepped into the waiting automobiles, and as the King and Queen with the Princesses drove off they were greeted with ringing cheers by the massed spectators.

The royal procession rolled into the streets of Southampton, gay with flags, bunting, and banners, and crowded with people shouting long cheers. At the Civic Centre, after a royal salute by a guard of honour of the Hampshire Territorials, the Mayor and Mayoress, Mr. and Mrs. A. H. Powdrill, greeted Their Majesties. After the inspection of the guard of honour, the royal party moved to a dais on which were assembled the members of the Southampton Corporation.

Leaving the Civic Centre, the King and Queen drove through streets jammed with people from whom surged incessant waves of cheers until the royal party disappeared into the flag-draped Central Station. Immediately the Sovereigns left in a special train on the last lap of their epoch-making voyage.

Meanwhile both Houses of Parliament had met in the afternoon. In the House of Commons the Prime Minister rose and said:

I beg to move,

That an humble Address be presented to His Majesty assuring His Majesty, on the occasion of his return from Canada, Newfoundland, and the United States of America, of the loyal and affectionate welcome of this House to His Majesty and Her Majesty the Queen.

Seven weeks ago, it was my privilege to move that an humble Address be presented to His Majesty on the eve of his departure for Canada with Her Majesty the Queen, assuring him of the affection and deep interest with which this House would follow their progress during their journey. At that time all of us anticipated that this memorable visit would be accompanied by scenes of the greatest enthusiasm. I think it is no exaggeration to say that the demonstrations of loyalty and affection by the crowds which flocked together to welcome Their Majesties at every point of their journey have exceeded the utmost expectations. Thanks to the Press and the radio and the news reels, we have been able to follow every detail of Their Majesties' progress almost as if we had been present ourselves. We have been able to see with our own eyes how in Canada, and in Newfoundland later on, the visit has demonstrated in a most impressive manner not only the significance of the Crown in the British Commonwealth of Nations, but how loyalty to the Crown in the abstract has been translated into a personal feeling of affection for Their Majesties, a feeling which has been generated by seeing the simple, kindly, and human qualities which we know are characteristic of our King and Queen.

When Their Majesties crossed the frontier of the United States, that magnificent welcome they received from the President and the American people outdistanced all precedents, and must have delighted Their Majesties' hearts. I am certain that it afforded profound gratification to Their Majesties' subjects throughout the Empire, and I can speak for the people of this country when I say that we have all been profoundly moved by the warmth of this greeting, which we acclaim both as a personal tribute to the King and Queen, and also as a striking proof of the sympathy and friendship which animate the feelings of the peoples of the United States and the United Kingdom.

Supported by the Deputy Leader of the Opposition, the motion was carried unanimously.

In the House of Lords, Earl Stanhope, First Lord of the Admiralty, moved the same motion as presented in the House of Commons. Referring to his forecast when Their Majesties departed that Canada and the United States would extend to them a warm welcome, he added:

I take no credit for having used those words. They were indeed inadequate to describe the personal triumph which Their Majesties have achieved. They came, they saw, they conquered, and a conquest, my lords, of which every one of their subjects may be truly proud.

Lord Snell supported the motion with a brief address. Stressing the quality of the reception extended to Their Majesties, he said:

> All of us were certain that from his own people in Canada His Majesty would receive a fervent and moving welcome. When they saw him and his gracious Queen upon their own soil and in their own cities, the almost mystical reverence that they had for his person and his position was increased by an element of glad surprise. They then realised that their King and Queen were not austere, unapproachable, superhuman personalities, but friendly, understanding, approachable, and almost gay human beings, who were the representatives of that bond of union, based upon order, freedom, and progress, which makes one people of the whole of the British Commonwealth of Nations.
>
> Only those of us who knew America and loved her well could rightly estimate the quality and the warmth of the unorganised, uncoerced, and entirely spontaneous welcome that Their Majesties would receive. Upon an occasion which allowed scope for hospitality and vociferous welcome the American people would never allow themselves to be beaten by any nation upon the earth.

After brief remarks by other speakers, the motion was agreed to *nemine contradicente*.

At 5:25 the royal locomotive glided into Waterloo Station ablaze with flags. On the red carpet banked with flowers stood awaiting the royal travellers Queen Victoria Eugenie of Spain, Princess Arthur of Connaught, Lady Patricia Ramsay, Princess Alice, Countess of Athlone, and the Earl of Athlone. The American Ambassador, the High Commissioner for Canada, and the Brazilian Ambassador were also present. The Prime Minister was accompanied by Mrs. Chamberlain. Other Cabinet Ministers and representatives of London were also in the group.

As the King stepped out to the platform, followed by the Queen and the Princesses, Their Majesties were greeted with three warm cheers from the distinguished assemblage. After the family greetings, the King and Queen shook hands with the Ministers of the Crown, the Ambassadors, and Mr. Vincent Massey. After a few minutes the King and Queen left the station and with the two Princesses entered the open landau for the drive to Buckingham Palace, accompanied by a mounted escort of the Life Guards.

As the royal landau emerged from the station, a great chorus of cheers greeted Their Majesties. From that moment, acclamations kept rising in successive waves, so that the ovation never ended. Visibly pleased with London's enthusiasm, the King raised his hand to the salute again and again, while the Queen repeatedly responded with her graceful wave of the hand.

When the royal procession reached Parliament Square, the King and Queen were greeted by members of both Houses of Parliament, present as a body, and lining the pavement, joining their hurrahs with the acclamations of the crowds.

Through Trafalgar Square and the Mall, massed ranks of spectators raised a deafening din of cheers and applause, until the royal landau rolled through the gates into the Palace quadrangle.

After Their Majesties had entered the Palace, the crowd of thousands raised the cry: 'We want the King! We want the Queen!' After a twenty-minute wait, the King and Queen came out onto the balcony with the two Princesses.

After Their Majesties had gone back into the Palace, the majority of the crowd waited hopefully for a new appearance of the royal couple. About two hours later, Their Majesties appeared once more on the balcony. Again they were loudly cheered as they waved for a few minutes to the crowd before re-entering the Palace at quarter past eleven. Finally, about half past eleven, the lights in the Palace began to be turned out, and the spectators moved away. That night, for the first time in seven weeks, the King and Queen slept in their own home again, at the end of a happy and wonderful journey.

EPILOGUE

The befitting epilogue to this spectacular journey was the luncheon given the next day, June 23, in honour of the King at the Guildhall by the Corporation of the City of London.

At half past twelve, the King, accompanied by the Queen, left Buckingham Palace in an open landau. The state procession of four carriages drove to the Guildhall with a Captain's escort of scarlet-coated Life Guards with Standard.

In his rich-crimson robe of office with cape of ermine, the Lord Mayor, with the Lady Mayoress, received with the traditional ceremonial the City's guests. These guests formed a most distinguished assemblage of national personalities. The general company having taken their places in the Great Hall, the trumpeters sounded a fanfare, and the King entered with the Lady Mayoress, and the Queen followed with the Lord Mayor. The general applause turned quickly into a rousing roar of cheering, and the band broke into the National Anthem.

Luncheon over, the Lord Mayor rose and gave the toast: 'Their Majesties the King and Queen'. The toast was honoured by the company, and all joined in the singing as the band played the National Anthem.

Rising again a few minutes later, the Lord Mayor said that he wished to express the feelings of all His Majesty's subjects, which were feelings of deep gratitude to the King and Queen for their historic journey and of great joy upon their return. Thanks to modern science, he added, it had been an 'exhilarating experience of hearing for ourselves the wonderful demonstrations of loyalty by our fellow subjects in Canada and Newfoundland, and the characteristically generous and warm-hearted reception accorded to Your Majesties in the United States of America.' Continuing, he said: 'We are gathered here today, amid the rejoicings of Your Majesty's subjects, to welcome Your Majesties on your return and to offer our humble congratulations on the success which has marked every stage of your journey.'

The Lord Mayor concluded his speech by reading the following cable he had received from the Prime Minister of Canada:

The citizens of Canada desire to join with the citizens of London and indeed of all parts of the British Empire in their rejoicings upon the safe return of the King and Queen after the voyage of Their Majesties across the Atlantic, and their visit to the New World. At no time has such a welcome been accorded a reigning Sovereign as that which marked the progress of King George and Queen Elizabeth across Canada, and Their Majesties' visits to the United States and Newfoundland. In the personalities and purpose of the King and Queen the peoples of the countries visited have found the expression of the ideals which they hold in common and which they long to see prevail. It will be the prayer of one and all that Their Majesties may long be spared to further among men and nations the understanding friendship and goodwill which, with such evident sincerity, they everywhere manifested, and on which, more than all else, depends the well-being of mankind throughout the world.

A fanfare of trumpets heralded the King's reply to the Lord Mayor:

I thank you, my Lord Mayor—I thank you, ladies and gentlemen—for the manner in which you have honoured this toast.

I thank you also for your recognition of the significance of the long journey that the Queen and I have just completed. To us personally it was a momentous and happy experience. Historically it was unique in that no reigning Sovereign has in time past entered one of the sister Dominions that constitute our British Empire. It is my earnest hope that it may also be of some importance in its influence on the Empire's future destiny.

We left these shores almost seven weeks ago. During that time we have travelled many thousands of miles by land and by sea; we have seen great cities, noble rivers, and vast mountain ranges; we have been welcomed, with a sincerity that stirred us profoundly, by millions of our fellow human beings, in Canada, in the United States of America, and in Newfoundland. In the last twenty-four hours that welcome has been re-echoed in the land which to us, as to so many of our kindred overseas, will always be home.

The detailed story of our travels is familiar to you through the daily press, the news reels, and the broadcasting corporations which, on both sides of the Atlantic, have reported it with accuracy and sympathetic understanding. I shall only try here today to tell you some of the impressions of my journey that remain in my mind.

The first, and deepest, is that, even in this age of machines and mass-production, the strength of human feeling is still the most potent of all the forces affecting world affairs. 'Over all nations'—as a North American historian has written—'over all nations is humanity.' In no part of the world, perhaps, is that truth more evident than in the continent from which I have just returned. With its geographical limits live men of almost every race, of many creeds, of divers political faiths; yet first and foremost they are human beings—over them all is humanity.

I found inspiration, too, in the realization that we in these islands have made a helpful contribution to the gradual weaving of that fabric of humanity. That is evident, of course, from the pages of history; but which of us has not found that history, and geography too, never really live for us until we travel? I was deeply impressed, for example, to find our great political testament, Magna Carta, an object of keen public interest in the World's Fair at New York, and at every turn of my long journey it was constantly brought home to me how closely interwoven are the threads of our own story with those of the development of that newer continent across the sea. Especially was this true in Canada. Were you, my Lord Mayor, to find yourself in the City Hall of Vancouver, you would see there, on the coast of the Pacific Ocean, some 6,000 miles from this Guildhall, an exact replica of the mace which, in this old City of London, is the symbol of your civic authority. The sight would stir the imagination of any man who holds your high and ancient office.

So it was with me. In Canada, I saw everywhere not only the mere symbol of the British Crown; I saw also, flourishing as strongly as they do here, the institutions which have developed, century after century, beneath the aegis of that Crown; institutions, British in origin, British in their slow and almost casual growth, which, because they are grounded root and branch on British faith in liberty and justice, mean more to us even than the splendour of our history or the glories of our English tongue.

To see them thus vigorous on Canadian soil could not but be a source of pride to me; and I counted it a high privilege to be the first of my line to play some personal part in giving them practical effect. In person I presided over the Canadian Parliament at Ottawa, and assented to Legislation; in person I received the credentials of the new Minister of Canada's great and friendly neighbour, the United States; in person I signed the Trade Treaty between the two countries.

And, even in the loyal enthusiasm shown to the Queen and myself by hundreds of thousands of my Canadian subjects, young and old, I thought I detected too the influence of those institutions. For it was not alone the actual presence of their King and Queen that made them open their hearts to us; their welcome, it seemed to me, was also an expression of their thankfulness for those rights of free citizenship which are the heritage of every member of our great Commonwealth of Nations.

It was the desire to serve the ideals of that Commonwealth which led me to undertake my journey; to foster its sane and wholesome faith; to show, if I could, that its headship, which I have been called upon to assume, exists today as a potent force for promoting peace and goodwill among mankind; these were the objects that I, and the Queen with me, set out to fulfil. It will be a source of thankfulness to us all our lives long if we have in some sort succeeded.

The City's reception having ended, the Lord Mayor and Lady Mayoress escorted Their Majesties to the royal landau. The return journey to Buckingham Palace witnessed another triumphant march. When the procession disappeared from view into the forecourt of the Palace, the crowd surged forward with a last rousing and warm-hearted cheer: the King and Queen had come home to stay.

Thus came to a close the greatest journey ever undertaken by a British Sovereign. Its conception by the Canadian Government was an inspiration; its execution by the King and Queen was perfection; and the most wonderful part of all was the people's overwhelming devotion.